THIRD EDITION

MORE
READING POWER 3

TEST BOOKLET

Linda Jeffries

Beatrice S. Mikulecky

More Reading Power 3 Test Booklet, Third Edition

Pearson Education, 10 Bank Street, White Plains, NY 10606

Staff credits: The people who made up the *More Reading Power 3 Test Booklet* team,
  representing editorial, production, design, and manufacturing, are Kim Casey, Dave Dickey,
  Ann France, Amy McCormick, Liza Pleva, and Mary Perrotta Rich.

Text credits: Page 16, From THE SCARECROW by Michael Connelly. Copyright © by Hieronymous, Inc.
  By permission of Little, Brown and Company. All rights reserved.
  Page 52, "Honor Thy Father and Thy Mother" Reprinted by permissions of The Wendy Weil Agency, Inc.
  First published in THE YALE REVIEW © 1972 by Judith Cerniak.
  Page 53, Excerpt from "The Hitchhiker," adapted from THE WONDERFUL WORLD OF HENRY SUGAR
  AND SIX MORE by Roald Dahl, copyright 1945, 1947, 1977 by Roald Dahl Nominee Limited. Used by
  permission of Alfred A. Knopf, an imprint of Random House Children's Books, a division of Random House,
  Inc. (E-Rights) Roald Dahl, "The Hitchhiker," The Wonderful Story of Henry Sugar and Six More. © David
  Higham Literary Agency. Reproduced by permission. All rights reserved.

Text composition: TSI Graphics
Text font: Times

ISBN 10: 0-13-208904-1

ISBN 13: 978-0-13-208904-3

CONTENTS

INTRODUCTION

This *Test Booklet* follows the format of the third edition of *More Reading Power 3*. It includes tests for Parts 2, 3, and 4. There are no tests for Part 1, because students' progress in extensive reading can best be evaluated with methods other than formal testing. These methods are discussed in the *Teacher's Guide*.

The introduction to each part of the test booklet includes a list of the tests in that Part. This list also provides the following information about the tests:

1. The corresponding exercise(s) in the Student Book

The tests are intended to follow work that students do in the Student Book. Teachers can give a test after students have completed the exercise in the Student Book that presents a given skill, strategy, or vocabulary set. Teachers should not give a test before students have completed the corresponding exercise.

2. The type of test: S = Skill/strategy, V = Vocabulary

S=Skills/strategies tests

The tests of skills and strategies reflect the approach taken in *More Reading Power 3*, where reading is viewed as a process involving many skills and strategies, including those necessary for learning vocabulary. (This approach is explained in detail in the *Teacher's Guide*.) The teacher's goals in testing students on their mastery of a skill or strategy should be 1) to verify how well students have understood the processes and 2) to evaluate their ability to put the skill or strategy to use in their reading or learning. Research has shown this can best be done by a test that reflects the format of the training. Therefore, the tests of this type are similar to the corresponding exercises in the Student Book.

In scoring tests of skills or strategies, teachers should keep in mind the aim of these tests and not simply look for the correct answer. In fact for many exercises, the responses given in the Answer Key should be considered those that are most likely, but not necessarily the only ones. Teachers should accept answers that differ from those in the Answer Key.

The tests of skills and strategies can also serve another purpose: further practice. According to the context and the level of the class, some teachers may find that their students (or some of them) need additional work in certain areas. This is the reason why two tests are included for some skills or strategies.

V=Vocabulary tests

These tests aim to assess students' knowledge of the words and phrases targeted in *More Reading Power 3* in some units of Part 2 and in the Focus on Vocabulary sections of each of the units of Part 3.

UNIT TESTS

PART 1: EXTENSIVE READING

As stated in the introduction to the test booklet, **students should NOT be tested in a formal way on their extensive reading.** Testing of comprehension or vocabulary would change the reading experience and could destroy a student's enjoyment of the story or book.

However, it is important for teachers to evaluate students' progress in their extensive reading. There are several reasons for this. First, teachers may need some measure of students' work in this part of the course. Second, evaluating their reading will reinforce the idea that students should take extensive reading seriously. And third, some of the methods for evaluation also allow students to communicate their experiences and share them with others.

Unit 3 of Part 1 includes several speaking and writing activities relating to extensive reading. Teachers will find others described in the Teacher's Guide on pages 11–14 or in the reference books listed in the Teacher's Guide.

Teachers should keep in mind, however, that evaluative activities can be overdone. Students who are often required to follow up their reading with exercises of one kind or another may come to dread finishing a book. Such exercises may seem like "busywork" to the students, without relevance to them and their reading experience.

Reading Targets

Teachers should make it clear to students that they will be expected to fulfill the basic aim of extensive reading—to read a lot. There are several ways to do this. The simplest is to establish a required number of books for all students.

Alternatively, to increase student involvement and motivation, teachers can talk with the class about how many books they think they can read in a semester, and then ask each student to write a target number in their Student Book; for example, at the top of the Reading Log on page 26. During the semester teachers should then check on students' progress with respect to their targets.

PART 2: VOCABULARY BUILDING

Introduction

As most teachers are aware, reading improvement and vocabulary expansion are closely related. To promote vocabulary development, *More Reading Power 3* includes both direct instruction of useful vocabulary items and instruction in vocabulary learning strategies. (The rationale behind the approach to vocabulary in *More Reading Power 3* is explained more fully in the Teacher's Guide.)

The tests in this part reflect these two types of instruction. Some focus on specific words or phrases presented in these units. Many other tests, however, assess students' acquisition of the strategies they need to become independent vocabulary learners. This is a key aspect of the approach to vocabulary in *More Reading Power 3*. For students to expand their vocabularies in a serious way, they must make a habit of selecting and learning vocabulary on their own.

Definitions—Which Language?

Until recently it was believed that students should use only English–English dictionaries, should always learn definitions in English, and should be tested in English. However, many experts, including Nation (2004), now believe this is not necessarily the most effective way for students to learn vocabulary. Intermediate-level students may learn vocabulary better with bilingual dictionaries and definitions in their own language because those definitions are more accessible and easier to remember. Students who wish to use bilingual dictionaries and to write definitions in their own language should therefore be allowed to do so in their notebooks and on study cards. If the teacher has a way to check on their work, they should also be allowed to use their language on vocabulary tests.

Notes:

- **Unit 2: Learning New Vocabulary from Your Reading**

  Tests 1 and 2: These do not test students in the usual way and cannot be graded like most tests since there are no right or wrong answers. These "tests" provide teachers with more exercises like those in the Student Book. Teachers can use them either for further practice or to evaluate how well students are able to follow the procedure for selecting and learning new words. Grades can be given as follows:
    A = Fully competent and autonomous in following procedure
    B = Mostly competent, with only occasional need for guidance
    C = Limited competence and frequent need for guidance
    D = Marginal competence and constant need for guidance
    F = Unable to follow procedure at all

  Test 3: This serves as a model for teachers to use for testing students on the words they have chosen. It is important for teachers to test students on these words so that students take the procedure seriously. Test 3 can be photocopied or copied by students onto a piece of paper. The format can be used repeatedly throughout the course to assess students' independent learning. Teachers should test students this way at the end of every unit of the Student Book. They can also ask students to select words or phrases from other readings (though not their extensive reading), and test them on those as well.

- **Unit 5: Collocations**

  Teachers who feel that these tests are too challenging and students will not be able to come up with the missing words on their own can make the tests easier by:

    1. providing all missing words for each test in a box (as in the corresponding exercises in the Student Book).
    2. providing the first letter of each missing word.

Part 2

List of Tests

	Type of Test*	Corresponding Exercise in Student Book		Type of Test*	Corresponding Exercise in Student Book
Unit 1			**Unit 5**		
Test 1	S	Exercise 5	Test 1	V	Examples and Practice
Test 2	S	Exercise 6	Test 2	V	Exercise 1
Test 3	S	Exercise 8	Test 3	V	Exercise 2
Test 4	S	Exercise 8	Test 4	V	Exercise 3
Unit 2			Test 5	V	Exercise 4
Test 1	S	Exercise 4	Test 6	V	Exercise 5
Test 2	S	Exercise 4	Test 7	V	Exercise 6
Test 3	V	Exercise 4	**Unit 6**		
Unit 3			Test 1	V	Exercise 1
Test 1	S	Exercise 4	Test 2	V	Exercise 3
Test 2	S	Exercise 4	Test 3	V	Exercise 4
Test 3	S	Exercise 6	Test 4	S	Exercise 5
Test 4	S	Exercise 8	Test 5	S	Exercise 6
Unit 4			Test 6	S	Exercise 8
Test 1	V	Exercise 5			
Test 2	V	Exercise 8			
Test 3	V	Exercise 12			
Test 4	V	Exercise 12			

*S = Skill or Strategy   V = Vocabulary

UNIT 1
Making Good Use of the Dictionary

TEST 1

Write the part of speech for each underlined word.

1. Max is a distant <u>relative</u> on my mother's side of the family.

   Part of speech: _____

2. The job must be in an area that <u>relates</u> to your degree.

   Part of speech: _____

3. <u>Relations</u> between aid workers and the population are difficult.

   Part of speech: _____

4. This issue is <u>related</u> to the question we discussed earlier.

   Part of speech: _____

5. Compared with the others, he is <u>relatively</u> unknown.

   Part of speech: _____

6. Shifra's <u>relationship</u> with her father was not a happy one.

   Part of speech: _____

re·late /rɪˈleɪt/ v. **1** [T] to show or prove a connection between two or more things: *I don't understand how the two ideas relate.* **2** [I] to be concerned with or directly connected to a particular subject: *How does this job relate to your career goals?* **3** [T] (formal) to tell someone about something that has happened: *He later related the whole story to us.*
relate to sb/sth phr. v. to understand how someone feels: *I find it hard to relate to kids.*

re·lat·ed /rɪˈleɪtɪd/ adj. **1** connected by similar ideas or dealing with similar subjects: *Police believe the murders are related.* | *Lung cancer and other diseases are related to smoking.* | *Politics and economics are closely related.*
2 stress-related/drug-related etc. caused by or relating to stress, drugs, etc.: *alcohol-related violence* **3** connected by a family relationship: *Are you related to Paula?*

re·la·tion /rɪˈleɪʃən/ n. **1 in relation to sb/sth** used when comparing two things or showing the relationship between them: *The area of land is tiny in relation to the population.* **2 relations** [plural] official connections and attitudes between countries, organizations, groups, etc.: *Are the relations between the staff and students good?* | *Israel's relations with its Arab neighbors* | *The U.S. has maintained diplomatic relations with Laos.* **3** [C,U] a connection between two things: *Is there any relation between the medication he was taking and his death?* | *This case bears no relation to (=is not connected with or similar to) the Goldman trial.* **4** [C] a member of your family **SYN** relative

re·la·tion·ship /rɪˈleɪʃənˌʃɪp/ n. **1** [C] the way in which two people or groups behave toward each other: *They seem to have a good relationship.* | *A mother's relationship with her children is important to their development.* | *In his speech, he mentioned the special relationship between the U.S. and Britain.* **2** [C] a situation in which two people have sexual or romantic feelings for each other: *a sexual relationship* | *He's much happier now that he's in a relationship.* **3** [C,U] the way in which two or more things are related to each other: *The study looked at the relationship between pay and performance at work.*

rel·a·tive¹ /ˈrɛlətɪv/ n. [C] a member of your family: *a close relative* (=mother, brother, cousin, etc.) | *distant relatives* (=second or third cousins, etc. that you rarely see)

relative² adj. **1** having a particular quality when compared with something else: *The 1950s were a time of relative peace/calm/prosperity for the country.* **2 relative to sth** relating to or compared with a particular subject: *Demand for corn is low relative to the supply.*

rel·a·tive·ly /ˈrɛlətɪvli/ adv. to a particular degree, especially when compared to something similar: *It's a relatively inexpensive restaurant.*

UNIT 1
Making Good Use of the Dictionary

TEST 2

Write the part of speech and definition for each underlined word as it is used in the sentence.

1. The bank <u>statement</u> showed that he had taken $20,000 out of his account.

   Part of speech: _____

   Definition: _____

   _____

2. Portland is the largest city in the <u>state</u> of Oregon.

   Part of speech: _____

   Definition: _____

   _____

3. All of his co-workers noticed that he was in a very negative <u>state</u> of mind.

   Part of speech: _____

   Definition: _____

   _____

4. The mayor <u>stated</u> that he knew nothing about the Swiss bank account.

   Part of speech: _____

   Definition: _____

   _____

5. In his <u>statement</u> to the police, he said that he was at home all evening.

   Part of speech: _____

   Definition: _____

   _____

6. Until the 1990s, the <u>State</u> controlled all of the Russian oil and gas industry.

   Part of speech: _____

   Definition: _____

   _____

state¹ /steɪt/ n. **1** [C] the condition that someone or something is in: *We are concerned about the state of the economy.* | *Exercise can improve your state of mind* (=the way you think and feel). | *They found him in a state of shock.* | *The house was in a sorry state* (=in a bad condition). **2** [C] *also* **State** POLITICS one of the areas with limited law-making powers that some countries, such as the U.S., are divided into: *the state of Oklahoma* **3** [C,U] *also* **State** POLITICS a country or its government: *a meeting between heads of state* | *state-owned industries*
4 the States (spoken) the U.S., used especially by someone when s/he is outside of the U.S. **5 a state of affairs** a situation: *It is a sad/sorry state of affairs when you can kill someone and only spend a year in jail.* **6 state visit/ceremony/opening etc.** POLITICS an important official visit, ceremony, etc. involving governments or rulers: *the President's state visit to Moscow* [ORIGIN: 1100—1200 Old French *estat*, from Latin *status*, from the past participle of *stare* "to stand"]

state² v. [T] (formal) **1** to give a piece of information or your opinion, especially by saying it clearly: *Please state your name.* | *The witness stated that he had never seen the woman before.*
2 if a document, ticket, etc. states information, it contains the information written clearly

ˌstate ˈline n. [C] the border between two states in the U.S.

state·ly /ˈsteɪtli/ adj. impressive in style or size: *a stately mansion*

state·ment /ˈsteɪtʰmənt/ n. [C] **1** something that you say or write officially and publicly: *The president is expected to make a statement later today.* | *the candidate's statement about/on the economy* | *He gave a statement to the police.* **2** ECONOMICS a list showing amounts of money paid, received, etc. and their total: *a bank statement* **3 make a statement** to do something, such as wear particular clothing or drive a particular type of car, in order that people will have a particular opinion of you: *Why get your nose pierced? Are you trying to make a statement?*

UNIT 1
Making Good Use of the Dictionary

TEST 3

Read the example phrases and sentences on the dictionary page in Test 1. Then complete each sentence. Use the part of speech given. (More than one answer is possible.)

1. Noun
   a. The early part of the century was a period of relative _____ for the area.

   b. _____ -related health problems are common among air traffic controllers.

2. Verb
   a. What he said _____ no relation to the situation.

3. Adjective
   a. They invited only their _____ relatives and a few friends to their wedding.

   b. He said he was a _____ relative, and I'd never met him before.

   c. _____ relations between the United States and China have improved lately.

   d. The plane ticket was relatively _____ for the summer season.

4. Adverb
   a. The Norwegian, Danish, and Swedish languages are _____ related, but not the same.

5. Preposition
   a. The relationship _____ the president and the vice president was tense.

   b. He had the same last name, but he was not related _____ the famous writer.

   c. The boy never had a good relationship _____ his father.

   d. The number of foreign students was small _____ relation _____ the whole student population.

UNIT 1
Making Good Use of the Dictionary

TEST 4

Read the example phrases and sentences on the dictionary page in Test 2. Then complete each sentence. Use the part of speech given. (In some sentences, more than one answer is possible.)

1. Noun

   a. Your state of _____ can influence your performance on a

      test.

   b. After the accident, she was in a state of _____ and could not

      answer questions.

   c. As a visiting _____ of state, he sat next to the U.S. President.

   d. What is the explanation for this state of _____?

   e. The _____ was stated in small print at the bottom of the

      document.

   f. He didn't state his _____ clearly until the end of the

      interview.

2. Verb

   a. The mayor will _____ a statement to the press later today.

   b. He went to the police station and _____ a statement in her

      defense.

3. Adjective

   a. Our poor little cat was in a very _____ state when we found

      her.

   b. In the Soviet Union, many industries were state-_____.

4. Preposition

   a. Millions of people listened to the President's statement _____

      the terrorist attacks.

UNIT 2
Learning New Vocabulary from Your Reading

TEST 1

A. Read the passage to the end. Do not stop to look up new words.

Ravens: Intelligent Birds

The raven is a large, black bird found in many areas of the world. It lives in all kinds of climates, from the arctic cold of Greenland to the desert heat of North Africa. This wide range is possible because ravens are very adaptable. They eat almost anything, including fruit, seeds, grains, insects, eggs, small animals and birds, and leftover food in garbage dumps.

In many cultures, people have included ravens in their stories and beliefs. Sometimes these birds are a symbol of death or evil. In medieval Sweden, for example, ravens were the ghosts of murdered people. In Denmark, an old story tells about ravens eating the king's heart and gaining terrible powers. In other cultures, however, ravens are seen more positively, as in some Native American cultures, where the god of creation is a raven.

What has impressed people about ravens in so many different cultures is their intelligence. Scientists have also been impressed and studies have confirmed that they are among the most intelligent species of birds. Many people have discovered this accidentally. A man who was hiking in the woods in Canada, for example, left his knapsack for a few minutes while he went to get wood for a fire. When he came back, he found the knapsack open, and his sunglasses, gloves, and other things on the ground. Nearby, a raven was finishing off his sandwich and two chocolate bars. In order to get the food, the raven had managed to open three zippers.

Along with intelligence, ravens are also known for their ability to work together towards a goal. This was demonstrated by a pair of ravens in Canada who had developed an effective system for stealing a meal from a dog on a chain. After the dog's owner brought its dinner, one of the ravens landed not far from the dog and began flapping its wings and making loud noises. The dog forgot about its dinner and ran to get the raven. But the raven had carefully calculated the distance and was just out of reach. While the dog barked and pulled at the chain, the second raven flew down behind it and began eating the dog's dinner. After a few minutes, the two ravens changed places. Once they had both eaten, they flew away.

Ravens usually make use of their intelligence to get food, but they are capable of solving other kinds of problems, too. In the Canadian Yukon, where winters can be extremely cold, some ravens made use of modern technology to survive the climate. The street lights there have light sensors that tell the lights to turn on when it is dark. Normally, the lights are off during the day, but the ravens discovered that if they sat on the lights and covered the sensors with their wings, the lights would turn on. Then the heat from the lights would warm them up.

(continued on next page)

B. Read the passage again. Underline the words and phrases that are new to you.

C. Look at the word list in the Student Book on pages 290–297 for the words and phrases you underlined. In the passage, circle the words that you find on the list.

D. Think about the underlined words that were not on the list. Are they useful? Circle the ones you want to learn. Then show them to your teacher.

E. Look up the circled words in the dictionary. Write the parts of speech and the definitions in the margin.

UNIT 2
Learning New Vocabulary from Your Reading

TEST 2

A. Read the passage to the end. Do not stop to look up new words.

The Hawaiian Islands

Like other islands in the Pacific Ocean, the Hawaiian Islands were formed by volcanoes. According to geologic evidence, they appeared relatively recently, about 30 million years ago.

The volcanoes began to form on the bottom of the Pacific Ocean. Movement far under the surface of the earth caused openings to form on the ocean floor and lava (hot, liquid rock) began to flow up through these openings. The lava slowly built up into mountains that eventually were tall enough to rise above the water and become islands. Altogether, the Hawaiian Islands include 132 islands, though some are very small.

According to geologists, the Hawaiian Islands are still evolving, as though they were living beings. The oldest islands, such as the Kure Atoll, are coming to the end of their existence. Over millions of years, they have gradually been worn down by the wind and the water, and they are slowly disappearing again under the waves. Now, nothing is left but a semicircle of coral reef (rock-like forms made by tiny sea animals).

On the other hand, the younger islands are still expanding. The Big Island of Hawaii has two active volcanoes that continue to send out lava, which flows down the mountains and hardens into rock. There are also new islands in the process of formation. One has been found about 30 miles south of the big island of Hawaii. Now about 3,000 feet below the ocean surface, geologists predict that it will eventually rise above the water and become another Hawaiian Island.

When each of the islands first appeared, it was bare rock, empty of life. Then the rock began to wear down and pockets of soil were created. The first species of plant life probably arrived as seeds, carried there by the wind or the ocean. They grew well in the rich, volcanic soil. Eventually, birds and insects were attracted to the islands, though this appearance of life all happened very gradually. Scientists believe, for example, the rate of change for plants was about one new species every 20,000 years.

Over time, the species of plants, birds, and insects became more numerous and more varied. They also gradually evolved, changing to adapt to the island conditions. That is why the Hawaiian Islands are home to so many species of plants and birds that exist nowhere else. With just a few exceptions, plants, birds, and insects were the only forms of life on the Hawaiian Islands until the arrival of humans, about 1,500 years ago.

The first people to settle there were Polynesians from the Marquesa Islands, thousands of miles to the southeast. Somehow they had learned about other islands to the north, perhaps from birds that flew north and never returned, or from pieces of wood that floated

(continued on next page)

south with the ocean currents. During a period of hard times, a group of Marquesans decided to sail north in search of these islands. They were excellent sailors, and so, using only the sun, the stars, the ocean currents, and the wind, at least some of their boats arrived successfully in Hawaii. They brought with them plants for farming and animals, such as goats and chickens. Their arrival meant the end of Hawaii's natural isolation.

B. Read the passage again. Underline the words and phrases that are new to you.

C. Look at the word list in the Student Book on pages 290–297 for the words and phrases you underlined. In the passage, circle the words that you find on the list.

D. Think about the underlined words that were not on the list. Are they useful? Circle the ones you want to learn. Then show them to your teacher.

E. Look up the circled words in the dictionary. Write the parts of speech and the definitions in the margin.

UNIT 2
Learning New Vocabulary from Your Reading

TEST 3

A. Write ten new words or phrases from your vocabulary notebook. Then close your notebook and write the meanings.

New Words/Phrases   Meanings

1. _____   _____

2. _____   _____

3. _____   _____

4. _____   _____

5. _____   _____

6. _____   _____

7. _____   _____

8. _____   _____

9. _____   _____

10. _____   _____

B. Now write sentences for four of the words from part A.

1. _____

2. _____

3. _____

4. _____

UNIT 3
Guessing Meaning from Context

TEST 1

Look for clues to the meaning of the underlined words or phrases in these sentences. Write the part of speech for each underlined word or phrase. Then make a guess about the general meaning.

1. From the animal's <u>skull</u>, the scientists could tell the shape of its head and the size of its brain.

   Part of speech: _____

   General meaning: _____

2. Suzanne's teachers were very <u>succinct</u> in their report to her parents. They had simply written: "A model student."

   Part of speech: _____

   General meaning: _____

3. After the tree was cut down, they <u>sawed</u> it into pieces that were the right length for the fireplace.

   Part of speech: _____

   General meaning: _____

4. Stone from the <u>quarry</u> in Stonington, Maine, was used to build many famous buildings, such as the Museum of Fine Arts in Boston.

   Part of speech: _____

   General meaning: _____

5. While she was waiting at the dentist's she <u>browsed through</u> a magazine, just looking at the pictures of famous people.

   Part of speech: _____

   General meaning: _____

6. My grandmother was a very <u>frugal</u> housewife. She was able to keep her home nice and make delicious meals, though she had very little money.

   Part of speech: _____

   General meaning: _____

UNIT 3
Guessing Meaning from Context

TEST 2

Look for clues to the meaning of the underlined words or phrases in these sentences. Write the part of speech for each underlined word or phrase. Then make a guess about the general meaning.

1. There were about 1,200 people <u>aboard</u> the *Titanic* when it hit an iceberg and sank.

    Part of speech: _____

    General meaning: _____

2. In spite of all the difficulties, the new president was able to <u>bring about</u> some important changes at the university.

    Part of speech: _____

    General meaning: _____

3. In some countries, shopkeepers expect to <u>haggle</u> with customers over prices and come to an agreement about the final cost of an item.

    Part of speech: _____

    General meaning: _____

4. I think there's a <u>leak</u> in this milk container. There's milk all over the bottom of the refrigerator.

    Part of speech: _____

    General meaning: _____

5. Those women work very hard and in difficult conditions. They <u>deserve</u> to be paid more.

    Part of speech: _____

    General meaning: _____

6. My friend Tom wants to move to the country and <u>breed</u> dogs. He says you can make a lot of money selling certain kinds of dogs.

    Part of speech: _____

    General meaning: _____

UNIT 3
Guessing Meaning from Context

TEST 3

Read the passages from *The Scarecrow,* by Michael Connelly, about a reporter for the *Los Angeles Times.* Use the context of the passages to figure out the part of speech and the general meaning of the underlined words and phrases. Circle the clues you use to make your guesses.

1. Twelve years earlier I'd had a short, intense, and, some would say, improper relationship with Rachel Walling. While I had seen photos of her in the papers a few years ago when she helped the LAPD (Los Angeles Police Department) run down and kill a wanted man in Echo Park, I had not been in her presence since we had sat in a hearing room (court room) nearly a decade earlier. Still, not many days went by in those ten years that I didn't think about her. She is one reason—perhaps the biggest reason—that I have always considered that time the high point of my life.

   She showed little <u>wear and tear</u> from the years that had passed, even though I knew it had been a tough time. She paid for her relationship with me with a five-year <u>stint</u> in a one-person office in South Dakota. She went from . . . chasing serial killers to investigating bar stabbings [injuries made with a knife] . . .

   a. *wear and tear*   Part of speech: _____

      General meaning: _____

   b. *stint*   Part of speech: _____

      General meaning: _____

2. But she had climbed out of that <u>pit</u> and had been (working) in L.A. for the past five years, working for some sort of secretive intelligence unit. I had called her when I'd found out, had gotten through to her but had been <u>rebuffed</u>. Since then I had <u>kept tabs on</u> her, when I could, from afar. And now she was standing in front of me in my hotel room in the middle of nowhere. It was strange, sometimes, how life worked out.

   a. *pit*   Part of speech: _____

      General meaning: _____

   b. *rebuffed*   Part of speech: _____

      General meaning: _____

   c. *kept tabs on*   Part of speech: _____

      General meaning: _____

UNIT 3
Guessing Meaning from Context

TEST 4

Use the context of the passages to figure out the part of speech and the general meaning of the missing words and phrases. Circle the clues you use to make your guesses.

1. In the 1930s, American farmers planted wheat in large areas of grassland in the south central United States. For a few years there was plenty of rain and lots of wheat. Then the rains stopped as they often do in this dry region. The wheat dried up and farming became impossible. The fields turned to xxxxxx, which blew away in great storms. The area became known as the "xxxxxx Bowl." What happened in the xxxxxx Bowl is a perfect example of erosion caused by modern farming methods. (Erosion is the loss of top soil, the top layer of earth.) Top soil blows away more easily when it is no longer protected by grasses or trees. In ten years or less, several feet of good soil can disappear. And once it is gone, there is no way to get it back quickly. It may take from one hundred to a thousand years for new top soil to form.

   Part of speech: _____

   Possible word or meaning: _____

2. In the twenty-first century, some American farmers are changing the way they farm. They have realized that the traditional methods are destructive of the environment, so they are trying different methods. First, they are no longer planting a single xxxxxx year after year over large areas of land. This has been the preferred system in the U.S. since the 1960s. Many farmers have planted only corn or only wheat for many years. But scientists—and farmers—now understand that planting the same xxxxxx year after year is not good for the soil. It is much better to plant several different xxxxxxs, and to change them every year.

   Part of speech: _____

   Possible word or meaning: _____

3. Another change for many farmers is that they xxxxxx much less and sometimes do not xxxxxx at all. Traditionally, the earth was xxxxxxed every year before planting time. Modern farm machinery can xxxxxx very deeply and turn over several feet of soil. However, studies have shown that this can lead to erosion. With no plants to hold it down, the soil washes away with the rain or blows away with the wind. The studies have also shown that when farmers xxxxxx deeply, they damage the quality of the soil, which becomes less productive.

   Part of speech: _____

   Possible word or meaning: _____

UNIT 4
Word Parts

TEST 1

Write the prefix, the root, and the meaning of the prefix. Then write the meaning of the word.

1. **uniform** (adj.)   Root: _____

   Prefix: _____   Meaning of prefix: _____

   Meaning of word: _____

2. **discourage**   Root: _____

   Prefix: _____   Meaning of prefix: _____

   Meaning of word: _____

3. **relive**   Root: _____

   Prefix: _____   Meaning of prefix: _____

   Meaning of word: _____

4. **overwork**   Root: _____

   Prefix: _____   Meaning of prefix: _____

   Meaning of word: _____

5. **outlive**   Root: _____

   Prefix: _____   Meaning of prefix: _____

   Meaning of word: _____

6. **bilingual**   Root: _____

   Prefix: _____   Meaning of prefix: _____

   Meaning of word: _____

7. **predate**   Root: _____

   Prefix: _____   Meaning of prefix: _____

   Meaning of word: _____

8. **miscalculate**   Root: _____

   Prefix: _____   Meaning of prefix: _____

   Meaning of word: _____

9. **nonprofit**   Root: _____

   Prefix: _____   Meaning of prefix: _____

   Meaning of word: _____

UNIT 4
Word Parts

TEST 2

Find the suffix in each word and circle it. Write the part of speech of the word. Then write the root and the part of speech of the root.

Word	Part of Speech	Root	Part of Speech of Root
1. likeable	_____	_____	_____
2. powerful	_____	_____	_____
3. modernization	_____	_____	_____
4. forgetfulness	_____	_____	_____
5. emotional	_____	_____	_____
6. prevention	_____	_____	_____
7. broaden	_____	_____	_____
8. personalize	_____	_____	_____
9. hopeful	_____	_____	_____
10. financially	_____	_____	_____
11. normally	_____	_____	_____
12. sensitive	_____	_____	_____
13. generalize	_____	_____	_____
14. weakness	_____	_____	_____
15. demanding	_____	_____	_____
16. truthful	_____	_____	_____
17. thoughtless	_____	_____	_____
18. confidently	_____	_____	_____
19. influential	_____	_____	_____
20. leading	_____	_____	_____

UNIT 4
Word Parts

TEST 3

Write the other forms for each word. (For some forms, more than one answer is possible.)

	Noun	Verb	Adjective	Negative Adjective	Adverb
1.		settle			X
2.					sensitively
3.	ability				
4.		popularize			
5.	rest				
6.	influence				X
7.				inconsiderate	
8.		value		X	X
9.			sure		
10.		develop			developmentally
11.	service			X	X
12.		depend			

UNIT 4
Word Parts

TEST 4

Write the other forms for each word. (For some forms, more than one answer is possible.)

	Noun	Verb	Adjective	Negative Adjective	Adverb
1.			formal		
2.					reportedly
3.	production				
4.			weak	X	
5.		believe			
6.	prediction				
7.		X		impossible	
8.	preparation				X
9.			simple	X	
10.		express			
11.				insubstantial	
12.			perfect		

UNIT 5
Collocations

TEST 1

Complete the collocation in each sentence with an appropriate word.

1. We thought the car key was lost forever, but it turned _____ after a week—in Peter's jacket pocket.

2. _____ the years, she got used to the spicy food and missed it when she went away.

3. _____ a moment. Please wait here. We'll tell you when you can go.

4. She speaks fluent English, German, and Turkish, and speaks excellent French as _____.

5. They had checked the map, but the town was even _____ than they thought. They had a long way to go.

6. When I pointed _____ that his smoke was bad for my health, the man finally put out his cigarette.

7. By the _____, have you heard the news about Sophie?

8. The concert _____ place in the garden behind an old house that is now the town library.

9. If you want to pass your Latin test, you have to know all the verb forms by _____.

10. At the party, she _____ into an old school friend she hadn't seen for years.

UNIT 5
Collocations

TEST 2

Complete the phrasal verb in each sentence with an appropriate preposition.

1. Work on the new buildings slowed _____ and then stopped completely because of financial problems.

2. Before you decide which car to buy, you should first figure _____ how much you can spend.

3. It was not a good time to have a guest in the house. There were just too many things going _____ in her life.

4. No one knew what brought _____ the change in his thinking.

5. Her work took _____ most of her time during the day, but she spent almost every evening with her mother.

6. Those who wish to take the entrance exams in September must sign _____ by the end of June.

7. Though it took a lot of time and was extremely boring, she carried _____ with the research.

8. It's not surprising that he's a researcher. Both his parents are biochemists and he was practically brought _____ at the lab.

UNIT 5
Collocations

TEST 3

Complete the collocation in each sentence with an appropriate word.

1. The severe *w*_____ of the past summer destroyed the crops of many farmers.

2. His wife says she's writing a book that will tell the full *s*_____ about their marriage. He's not going to be very happy about that.

3. One technological *i*_____ that changed history was the discovery of the wheel.

4. In developed countries, people eat meat, fish, and dairy products to get protein. But another cheap *s*_____ of protein in developing countries is insects.

5. The journalist, who was in close *c*_____ with the police, arrived at the crime scene very soon after the murder.

6. Young people today can find new *o*_____ in many areas of science and technology, such as in the development of new materials.

7. Anyone who saw the dramatic *s*_____ of the buildings burning would never forget it.

8. The death of his dog was a terrible *s*_____ to the old man.

UNIT 5
Collocations

TEST 4

Complete the collocation in each sentence with an appropriate preposition.

1. In her position _____ president of the company, she had to make a public statement.

2. His lack _____ experience was the main reason he did not get the job.

3. This player is much taller, which gives him an advantage _____ the other player.

4. His father had some doubts _____ Jonah's travel plans, but he did not say anything.

5. If you think your application was unfairly judged, you have a right _____ a review by a special committee.

6. One problem _____ the new system is that it's very slow.

7. Because of growing interest _____ the topic, another meeting is planned for next month.

8. There is a limit _____ everything! This is absolutely not acceptable.

UNIT 5
Collocations

TEST 5

Complete the collocation in each sentence with a verb in the appropriate form.

1. When he lost his job, he _____ a chess club and spent many hours there every day.

2. The students are organizing a concert to _____ money for the homeless families in town.

3. A healthy diet can _____ a big difference in an athlete's performance.

4. After the death of his father, he _____ charge of the farm.

5. While my mother was working, my grandmother used to _____ care of us.

6. He continued to _____ the family business when he was eighty years old.

7. Many foreigners in this country do not _____ access to good legal advice.

8. The company has _____ good progress toward completion of the new factory.

UNIT 5
Collocations

TEST 6

Complete the collocation in each sentence with an appropriate word. More than one answer may be possible. (Verbs should be in the correct form.)

1. In his lecture, he *r*_____ several key issues about politics in the Middle East today.

2. The results *s*_____ that current theories may need to be revised.

3. The paper discusses a *n*_____ of reasons for this strange phenomenon.

4. In order to *c*_____ out the research, she needed funds and an assistant.

5. They *s*_____ up the computer and printer in the living room where everyone one could use it.

6. In spite of computers and the Internet, we still use a great *d*_____ of paper.

7. The doctor said that the medicine has had no *e*_____ on his condition.

8. The teacher said he thought he could *d*_____ with a large class, but only if there were no difficult children.

UNIT 5
Collocations

TEST 7

Complete the collocation in each sentence with an appropriate word. More than one answer may be possible. (Verbs should be in the correct form.)

1. The bank's new rules *s*_____ a key purpose: to prevent people from borrowing money that they could not pay back.

2. The continuing political crisis was the *m*_____ reason for the country's economic problems.

3. Right now, we should *f*_____ on the important matters. All the rest can wait until later.

4. His experiences in Africa have *d*_____ changed his political views.

5. There has been no new research into this issue in *r*_____ years.

6. *A*_____ to the project director, it will take two years to complete all the research.

7. At the time, no one believed him, but in the long *r*_____, his theories were proved to be correct.

8. The results of the experiment showed *l*_____ difference between the two groups of people.

UNIT 6
Structure and Reference

TEST 1

Underline the subject(s) and verb(s) in each sentence in the passages. Write S under the subjects and V under the verbs.

Problems with Pensions

The developed countries today are all facing a similar economic problem: how to pay the pensions of retired people. The problem is basically the result of changes in the population. Thanks to improved health and medical care, more people are living longer. This has increased the amount the government must spend on pensions. At the same time, the birth rate has gone down, so there are fewer young people working and paying taxes. Therefore, there has been a significant reduction in revenue for the government. Other economic problems have further reduced spending money for most governments. In many of these countries, young people today wonder what—if any—pension they will receive when they retire.

Products and Services for Older Customers

In many of the developed countries, the population is aging. That is, the average age of the population is older than it was twenty years ago. This fact has encouraged many businesses to develop products and services for older customers. In the medical industry, for example, new medicines and technologies have been developed especially for the health problems of older people. The tourist industry has also begun to offer services for the elderly, including special transportation and trips organized for groups of older people. Finally, there are many different kinds of products designed for the needs of this part of the population, including everything from shoes and shampoos to magazines and furniture.

UNIT 6
Structure and Reference

TEST 2

Underline the signal words and phrases in the passage.

The Invasion of Alien Species

In many parts of the world, alien species are damaging the environment. An alien species is a plant or animal that has moved from its original home to a new area. Though some alien species may not cause any problems, others find perfect growing conditions and have no natural enemies, and so they grow and multiply without limit. Over time—sometimes decades, sometimes a few years—the new species takes the place of the native plants or animals. This can lead to dramatic changes in the natural landscape and various kinds of problems.

In some cases, people have purposely introduced the new species, unaware of possible future consequences. In 1876, for example, the Japanese government brought some Asian kudzu vine to show Americans in Philadelphia at the Centennial Exposition. Planted in gardens, this extremely fast-growing vine soon got out of control. Since then it has destroyed gardens, parks, trees, and forests all over the southern United States.

On the other hand, many alien species have been introduced accidentally, as a side effect of international trade. The Asian tiger mosquito, for example, probably traveled to Europe by ship in car tires filled with water. It has now largely replaced the common European mosquito in much of Italy, Spain, Greece, and southern France. Though the tiger mosquito has not so far caused disease in humans, it is very aggressive and the bites are unpleasant.

Another accidentally introduced species is the zebra mussel in the Great Lakes of North America. This small shellfish may have come over from Russia on a cargo ship. In just a few years, zebra mussels have spread through the lakes and into many important rivers. They form enormous masses, covering lake and river bottoms. Those masses take away food and oxygen from the native shellfish and fish. They also cut off water supplies for power stations and water treatment centers. Altogether, according to government officials, the mussels have caused many millions of dollars' worth of damage.

These days, scientists and governments are very aware of the possible negative consequences of introducing new species. Consequently, many countries, such as the United States, have strict rules about importing plants and animals. The Japanese government would never be allowed to bring in the kudzu vine today. However, as long as international trade continues, the risk of accidental introductions will also continue.

UNIT 6
Structure and Reference

TEST 3

Underline the personal pronouns and possessive adjectives. Write S under the subject pronouns, O under the object pronouns, and P under the possessive adjectives.

Ravens: Intelligent Birds

The raven is a large, black bird found in many areas of the world. It lives in all kinds of climates, from the arctic cold of Greenland to the desert heat of North Africa. This wide range is possible because ravens are very adaptable. They eat almost anything, including fruit, seeds, grains, insects, eggs, small animals and birds, and leftover food in garbage dumps.

In many cultures, people have included ravens in their stories and beliefs. Sometimes these birds are a symbol of death or evil. In medieval Sweden, for example, ravens were the ghosts of murdered people. In Denmark, an old story tells about ravens eating the king's heart and gaining terrible powers. In other cultures, however, ravens are seen more positively, as in some Native American cultures, where the god of creation is a raven.

What has impressed people about ravens in so many different cultures is their intelligence. Scientists have also been impressed and studies have confirmed that they are among the most intelligent species of birds. Many people have discovered this accidentally. A man who was hiking in the woods in Canada, for example, left his knapsack for a few minutes while he went to get wood for a fire. When he came back, he found the knapsack open, and his sunglasses, gloves, and other things on the ground. Nearby, a raven was finishing off his sandwich and two chocolate bars. In order to get the food, the raven had managed to open three zippers.

Along with intelligence, ravens are also known for their ability to work together toward a goal. This was demonstrated by a pair of ravens in Canada who had developed an effective system for stealing a meal from a dog on a chain. After the dog's owner brought its dinner, one of the ravens landed not far from the dog and began flapping its wings and making loud noises. The dog forgot about its dinner and ran to get the raven. But the raven had carefully calculated the distance and was just out of reach. While the dog barked and pulled at the chain, the second raven flew down behind it and began eating the dog's dinner. After a few minutes, the two ravens changed places. Once they had both eaten, they flew away.

(continued on next page)

Ravens usually make use of their intelligence to get food, but they are capable of solving other kinds of problems, too. In the Canadian Yukon, where winters can be extremely cold, some ravens made use of modern technology to survive the climate. The street lights there have light sensors that tell the lights to turn on when it is dark. Normally, the lights are off during the day, but the ravens discovered that if they sat on the lights and covered them with their wings, the lights would turn on. Then the heat from the lights would warm them up.

UNIT 6
Structure and Reference

TEST 4

Circle the referent for each underlined demonstrative pronoun or adjective. Then draw a line from the referent to the underlined word.

The Invasion of Alien Species

In many parts of the world, alien species are damaging the environment. An alien species is a plant or animal that has moved from its original home to a new area. Though some alien species may not cause any problems, others find perfect growing conditions and have no natural enemies, and so they grow and multiply without limit. Over time—sometimes decades, sometimes a few years—the new species takes the place of the native plants or animals. This
1.
can lead to dramatic changes in the natural landscape and various kinds of problems.

In some cases, people have purposely introduced the new species, unaware of possible future consequences. In 1876, for example, the Japanese government brought some Asian kudzu vine to show Americans in Philadelphia at the Centennial Exposition. Planted in gardens, this extremely fast-growing vine soon got out of control. Since then it has
2.
destroyed gardens, parks, trees, and forests all over the southern United States.

On the other hand, many alien species have been introduced accidentally, as a side effect of international trade. The Asian tiger mosquito, for example, probably traveled to Europe by ship in car tires filled with water. It has now largely replaced the common European mosquito in much of Italy, Spain, Greece, and southern France. Though the tiger mosquito has not so far caused disease in humans, it is very aggressive and the bites are unpleasant.

Another accidentally introduced species is the zebra mussel in the Great Lakes of North America. This small shellfish may have come over from Russia on a cargo ship.
3.
In just a few years, zebra mussels have spread through the lakes and into many important rivers. They form enormous masses, covering lake and river bottoms. Those masses take
4.
away food and oxygen from the native shellfish and fish. They also cut off water supplies for power stations and water treatment centers. Altogether, according to government officials, the mussels have caused many millions of dollars' worth of damage.

Today, scientists and governments are very aware of the possible negative consequences of introducing new species. In fact, many countries, such as the United States, have strict rules about importing plants and animals. The Japanese government would not be allowed now to bring in the kudzu vine. However, as long as international trade continues, the risk of accidental introductions will also continue.

UNIT 6
Structure and Reference

TEST 5

Underline the relative pronouns (*who, which, that, where*) in the passage. Then circle the referent and draw a line to the pronoun. (Remember: *that* can also be a demonstrative pronoun.)

Chimpanzee Behavior

A band, or group, of chimpanzees, which usually contains six to ten members, exists as part of a larger community of bands. These bands, the size of which may depend on the food available, may exchange members, join together, or divide up. Some bands are made up of young adult males, others of mothers and young chimpanzees. Membership in the bands is not fixed permanently, and individual chimpanzees come and go freely within the larger community.

Chimpanzees spend most of their lives in trees, where they sleep and find the fruits that are their main source of food. They also find some food on the ground—leaves, roots and other vegetable matter, as well as insects and, occasionally, small animals. But they rarely go far from a tree that they can climb to safety if they need to.

The long arms of the chimpanzee are good for swinging through trees, which is one way they get around the forest. However, they can also travel on the ground. Normally when they walk, they use both feet and "arms." They can also walk using only their legs, but just for short distances when they are carrying something in their hands. Chimpanzees are not able to swim and have no way of crossing large bodies of water.

When male chimpanzees are excited, they often stand on their legs and make loud noises. They may also throw things or attack, but this is less common. Female chimpanzees have a new baby every two or three years. The young chimpanzees, who stay close to their mothers for a number of years, are full size at about twelve years old. They spend more and more time with other young members of their band, and usually move to another band when they are adults.

UNIT 6
Structure and Reference

TEST 6

Find synonyms or related words in the passage. Follow these instructions:

  If a word is underlined, underline the synonyms and related words.

  If a word is circled, circle the synonyms and related words.

  If a word is boxed, box the synonyms and related words.

White Water Rafting

People who are looking for outdoor adventure often go to <u>Maine</u>. This state in the northeastern United States contains large areas of wilderness and many rivers suitable for white water (rafting).

On a rafting trip, you travel down a river on a flat rubber boat. In the past, this sport was practiced only in the western states, but now several outdoor travel companies offer weekend rafting trips in Maine. They provide guide service, equipment—including the rafts—and even food, and they welcome people who have no experience at all. Thus, city residents, too, can get a taste of the wilderness. All they need to bring with them is a desire for adventure.

"<u>White water</u>" is the water of a river when it moves very fast over rocks. These areas are the most exciting for rafters—and also the most dangerous. Rafting guides must always be looking out for white water and (rafters) must be ready to swim because the raft can tip over. For that reason, people on rafts must always wear special life vests that will keep them afloat.

Since these rafting trips are always downriver, rafters can relax and enjoy the scenery when the river is calm. There are deep, dark forests of evergreen trees, lovely open meadows with blueberries, and high mountains, too. However, if the river becomes rough, the rafters must pay more attention. Guiding the raft in rocky (areas) requires some skill. Strength, too, is required for the very rocky parts of a river that are impassible with a raft. Then everyone has to get out, and the rafts and all the equipment have to be carried to a smoother part of the river.

PART 3: COMPREHENSION SKILLS

Introduction

In *More Reading Power 3,* reading comprehension is viewed as a complex process that involves a variety of skills. These include "bottom up" decoding skills, such as recognizing letters and words, matching letters/words with sounds, and following syntax, as well as "top-down" thinking skills, such as identifying topics, main ideas and patterns of organization, applying background knowledge and logic, and making inferences. (This approach is explained more fully in the Teacher's Guide.)

In grading students' answers to these tests, teachers should keep in mind that the skills and strategies are part of a thinking process. Teachers should not simply look for "correct" answers. They should look for proof that students have understood and mastered the skill or strategy. As mentioned in the Introduction to Part 2, **teachers should accept answers that are different from those given in the Answer Key if students can justify them.**

The units in this part include exercises that require students to write phrases or sentences for the answers. Evaluating these will require more time and effort on the part of the teacher than with multiple choice questions, but the open-ended answers will also allow teachers to get a better sense of students' thinking processes.

Focus on Vocabulary sections:

For each of the Focus on Vocabulary sections in the Student Book, there are two tests of the target vocabulary. Teachers are advised **not to give students these tests immediately after completing a section**. Instead, the first test should be given after a few days or a week, and the second test after another week or two. In this way, they will serve as further reinforcement of the words and phrases and will support students' learning of them.

Part 3

List of Tests

	Type of Test*	Corresponding Exercise in Student Book		Type of Test*	Corresponding Exercise in Student Book
Unit 1			Test 10	S	Exercise 11
Test 1	S	Exercise 4	Test 11	S	Exercise 11
Test 2	S	Exercise 4	Test 12	S	Exercise 11
Test 3	S	Exercise 5	FOV Test 1**	V	FOV Exercise 6
Test 4	S	Exercise 5	FOV Test 2†	V	FOV Exercise 6
Test 5	S	Exercise 9	**Unit 4**		
Test 6	S	Exercise 10	Test 1	S	Exercise 9
FOV Test 1**	V	FOV Exercise 6	Test 2	S	Exercise 9
FOV Test 2†	V	FOV Exercise 6	Test 3	S	Exercise 9
Unit 2			Test 4	S	Exercise 9
Test 1	S	Exercise 2	FOV Test 1**	V	FOV Exercise 6
Test 2	S	Exercise 4	FOV Test 2†	V	FOV Exercise 6
Test 3	S	Exercise 4	**Unit 5**		
Test 4	S	Exercise 7	Test 1	S	Practice 2
Test 5	S	Exercise 8	Test 2	S	Exercise 2
FOV Test 1**	V	FOV Exercise 6	Test 3	S	Exercise 4
FOV Test 2†	V	FOV Exercise 6	Test 4	S	Exercise 6
Unit 3			Test 5	S	Exercise 6
Test 1	S	Exercise 2	FOV Test 1**	V	FOV Exercise 6
Test 2	S	Exercise 2	FOV Test 2†	V	FOV Exercise 6
Test 3	S	Exercise 5	**Unit 6**		
Test 4	S	Exercise 5	Test 1	S	Exercise 1
Test 5	S	Exercise 5	Test 2	S	Exercise 4
Test 6	S	Exercise 7	Test 3	S	Exercise 6
Test 7	S	Exercise 7	Test 4	S	Exercise 6
Test 8	S	Exercise 7	FOV Test 1**	V	FOV Exercise 6
Test 9	S	Exercise 11	FOV Test 2†	V	FOV Exercise 6

*S = Skill or Strategy   V = Vocabulary

** This test should be given about a week after completing the FOV section.

† This test should be given about two weeks after completing the FOV section.

UNIT 1
Scanning and Previewing

TEST 1   Scanning for information

A. Read the questions. Then scan the article on the next page and underline the answers. You will have three minutes.

1. What is the current population of Hawaii?

2. What is the name of the professor mentioned in the article?

3. About how many pure Hawaiians are alive now?

4. What Asian communities are mentioned?

5. Which is the largest ethnic group on the islands?

6. What percentage of native Hawaiians died between 1778 and 1878?

B. Write three more questions about the article. Then ask another student to scan for the answers.

_____

_____

_____

C. Discuss these questions with a partner.

1. Is there more than one ethnic group where you live now? If so, what are some of the groups?

2. If you grew up somewhere else, was that place multiethnic? If so, what groups lived there?

3. Have you ever participated in any events or holidays that are typical of another ethnic group? If so, what are they?

The People of Hawaii

In 1778, when the first European, Captain James Cook, arrived at the Hawaiian Islands, the native population was between 300,000 and 400,000. Over the course of the next one hundred years, that population dropped dramatically. About 80% of the native Hawaiians on the islands died, mostly from diseases introduced by Europeans and Americans.

By 1878, the native population on the islands had fallen to about 40,000. It was still the largest ethnic group, but as people began moving to Hawaii in large numbers, the percentage of native Hawaiians went down. One growing group was made up of white Americans and Europeans. Other groups were formed of Asian workers and their families who came to work on Hawaii's sugar plantations. Soon there were large communities of Japanese, Chinese, Filipinos, and people from South Pacific islands.

During the twentieth century, the number of pure Hawaiians (those with only Hawaiian blood) continued to decline. At present, there are less than 8,000 pure Hawaiians alive. On the other hand, the number of those who are part Hawaiian and who consider themselves to be Hawaiian, has increased to around 250,000, about 21% of the current population (about 1,211,500).

This part of the population—native Hawaiian or part Hawaiian—is the largest ethnic group on the islands. In fact, Hawaii is unique among the states of the United States. It is the only state where whites do not form a majority, and are not even the largest ethnic group. Indeed, they make up little more than 20% of the population. The rest of the population is made up of ethnic Asians and a small number of blacks.

These statistics, however, are only approximate, since many Hawaiians (almost half) identify themselves as belonging to more than one race or ethnic group. A significant percentage (about 20%) say they belong to two or more groups.

Some Hawaiians think that the multicultural and multiracial character of Hawaiian society could serve as a model for the rest of the United States. University of Hawaii professor Dan Boylan believes that this is the reason for the relative lack of racial conflict in the state. In Hawaii, different groups get along because none of them has a majority and none dominate. Anyone who wants to win elections in the state has to appeal to different ethnic groups. In order to govern, they must have support that goes across ethnic lines.

UNIT 1
Scanning and Previewing

TEST 2   Scanning for information

A. Read the questions. Then scan the article on the next page and underline the answers. You will have three minutes.

1. What is the world's record low temperature?

2. How thick is the ice on average in Antarctica?

3. How high are the mountains in Antarctica?

4. What land mammals are found in the Arctic?

5. What plants grow in Antarctica?

6. How much colder is Antarctica compared with the Arctic?

B. Write three more questions about the article. Then ask another student to scan for the answers.

_____

_____

_____

C. Discuss these questions with your partner.

1. Have you ever lived or traveled to an extremely cold place? If so, where?

2. Have you ever seen any of the animals mentioned in the passage? If so, where?

3. Have you heard anything about the effects of global warming on Antarctica or the Arctic? If so, what do you know about this topic?

Polar Opposites

The name Antarctica was given to the area around the South Pole because it means "opposite to the Arctic." It is in fact very different from the Arctic in many ways. Antarctica is a high, ice-covered landmass that is larger than the United States. The Arctic, on the other hand, is ice-covered ocean, with landmasses grouped around it.

Because of this geographical difference, the climate of the two areas is also very different. Antarctica is the coldest area in the world, colder than the Arctic by an average of 30 degrees. The interior (middle) is mountainous, with peaks nearly 10,000 feet (3,050 meters) high. In this area temperatures below −100 F (−73° C) are not uncommon. The world's record low temperature of −127° F (−88° C) was measured there in August 1960. Only in coastal regions do temperatures sometimes rise above freezing in the summer (December to March). In contrast, near the North Pole temperatures often rise above freezing in summer.

Due to the extreme cold, Antarctica is mostly covered with ice—4.5 million square miles of ice (7.24 million square km). This is about 85% of the total supply of ice on the planet. The ice is very thick, averaging nearly 8,000 feet (2,438 meters). Some of it has formed massive rivers of ice, called glaciers, which move very slowly down the mountains towards the ocean.

The ice at the Arctic, in contrast, covers ocean water and is generally not as thick. The thickness varies according to the time of year, as ice forms in winter and melts in summer. In recent years, more ice has melted than has reformed each year, and the total area covered by ice has become noticeably smaller, probably due to global warming.

The two polar regions are both home to plants and animals, but different ones. On the continent of Antarctica, there are very few plants. Only very small plants such as mosses, lichens, and algae can survive the extreme cold. The cold also makes the interior of Antarctica unlivable for animals, except for some kinds of insects. Among the kinds of wildlife that live on the coast, there are penguins, seals, whales, and many kinds of birds.

Unlike Antarctica, the landmasses in the Arctic are home to a number of kinds of plants, including small bushes, grasses, and herbs, as well as lichens and mosses. While the Arctic has no penguins, it does have many other kinds of birds, as well as marine (ocean) mammals such as seals, walruses, and whales. It also has many land mammals, including large ones such as polar bears, reindeer, and foxes, and small ones such as mice and lemmings.

In spite of these differences between the South and North Poles, and in spite of the enormous distance between them, some species of birds and whales live in both places and travel back and forth every year.

UNIT 1
Scanning and Previewing

TEST 3   Scanning for key words

Scan the article for the key words. Scan for one word at a time and circle that word every time you find it. Then write the number of times you found each key word.

Key word	Number of times
a. Hawaii(an)	_____
b. population	_____
c. native	_____
d. ethnic	_____
e. group	_____

The People of Hawaii

In 1778, when the first European, Captain James Cook, arrived at the Hawaiian Islands, the native population was between 300,000 and 400,000. Over the course of the next one hundred years, that population dropped dramatically. About 80% of the native Hawaiians on the islands died, mostly from diseases introduced by Europeans and Americans.

By 1878, the native population on the islands had fallen to about 40,000. It was still the largest ethnic group, but as people began moving to Hawaii in large numbers, the percentage of native Hawaiians went down. One growing group was made up of white Americans and Europeans. Other groups were formed of Asian workers and their families who came to work on Hawaii's sugar plantations. Soon there were large communities of Japanese, Chinese, Filipinos, and people from South Pacific Islands.

During the twentieth century, the number of pure Hawaiians (those with only Hawaiian blood) continued to decline. At present, there are less than 8,000 pure Hawaiians alive. On the other hand, the number of those who are part Hawaiian and who consider themselves to be Hawaiian, has increased to around 250,000, about 21% of the current population (about 1,211,500).

This part of the population—native Hawaiian and part Hawaiian—is the largest ethnic group on the islands. In fact, Hawaii is unique among the states of the United States. It is the only state where whites do not form a majority, and are not even the largest ethnic group. Indeed, they make up little more than 20% of the population. The rest of the population is made up of ethnic Asians and a small number of blacks.

These statistics, however, are only approximate, since many Hawaiians (almost half) identify themselves as belonging to more than one race or ethnic group. A significant percentage (about 20%) say they belong to two or more groups.

Some Hawaiians think that the multicultural and multiracial character of Hawaiian society could serve as a model for the rest of the United States. University of Hawaii professor Dan Boylan believes that this is the reason for the relative lack of racial conflict in the state. In Hawaii, different groups get along because none of them has a majority and none dominate. Anyone who wants to win elections in the state has to appeal to different ethnic groups. In order to govern, they must have support that goes across ethnic lines.

UNIT 1
Scanning and Previewing

TEST 4   Scanning for key words

Scan the article for the key words. Scan for one word at a time and circle that word
every time you find it. Then write the number of times you found each key word.

Key word	Number of times
a. Antarctica	_____
b. Arctic	_____
c. area(s)	_____
d. temperature(s)	_____
e. ice	_____

Polar Opposites

The name Antarctica was given to the area around the South Pole because it means
"opposite to the Arctic." It is in fact very different from the Arctic in many ways.
Antarctica is a high, ice-covered landmass that is larger than the United States. The Arctic,
on the other hand, is ice-covered ocean, with landmasses grouped around it.

Because of this geographical difference, the climate of the two areas is also very
different. Antarctica is the coldest area in the world, colder than the Arctic by an average
of 30 degrees. The interior (middle) is mountainous, with peaks nearly 10,000 feet (3,050
meters) high. In this area, temperatures below –100 F (–73° C) are not uncommon. The
world's record low temperature of –127° F (–88° C) was measured there in August 1960.
Only in coastal regions do temperatures sometimes rise above freezing in the summer
(December to March). In contrast, near the North Pole temperatures often rise above
freezing in summer.

Due to the extreme cold, Antarctica is mostly covered with ice—4.5 million square
miles of ice (7.24 million square km). This is about 85% of the total supply of ice on the
planet. The ice is very thick, averaging nearly 8,000 feet (2,438 meters). Some of it has
formed massive rivers of ice, called glaciers, which move very slowly down the mountains
towards the ocean.

The ice at the Arctic, in contrast, covers ocean water and is generally not as thick. The
thickness varies according to the time of year, as ice forms in winter and melts in summer.
In recent years, more ice has melted than has reformed each year, and the total area
covered by ice has become noticeably smaller, probably due to global warming.

The two polar regions are both home to plants and animals, but different ones. On the continent of Antarctica, there are very few plants. Only very small plants such as mosses, lichens, and algae can survive the extreme cold. The cold also makes the interior of Antarctica unlivable for animals, except for some kinds of insects. Among the kinds of wildlife that live on the coast, there are penguins, seals, whales, and many kinds of birds.

Unlike Antarctica, the landmasses in the Arctic are home to a number of kinds of plants, including small bushes, grasses, and herbs, as well as lichens and mosses. While the Arctic has no penguins, it does have many other kinds of birds, as well as seals, walruses and whales. It also has many land mammals, including large ones such as polar bears, reindeer, and foxes, and small ones such as mice and lemmings.

In spite of these differences between the South and North Poles, and in spite of the enormous distance between them, some species of birds and whales live in both places and travel back and forth every year.

UNIT 1
Scanning and Previewing

TEST 5   Previewing

A. Work with another student. Read the title of the article. Then write three previewing questions on a separate piece of paper.

B. Preview the text quickly and look for the answers to your previewing questions.

The Iceman

On a September day in 1991, two Germans were climbing the mountains between Austria and Italy. High up on a mountain pass, they found the body of a man lying on the ice. At that height (10,499 feet, or 3,200 meters), the ice is usually permanent, but 1991 had been an especially warm year. The mountain ice had melted more than usual and so the body had come to the surface.

It was lying face downward. The skeleton was in perfect condition, except for a wound on the back of his head. There was still skin on the bones and the remains of some clothes. The hands were holding the wooden handle of an ax and on the feet there were very simple leather and cloth boots. Nearby was a pair of gloves made of tree bark and a holder for arrows.

Who was this man? How and when had he died? In the first months after his discovery, many thought they had the answer to these questions. A Swiss woman believed it might be her father, who had died in those mountains twenty years before and whose body had never been found. Others thought that it was from earlier in the twentieth century, perhaps the body of a soldier who had died in World War I, since several soldiers had been found in the area.

However, the scientists who rushed to look at the body realized immediately that it was much older. To study it better, they needed to bring the body down the mountain to their laboratories. The question was, who did it belong to? It was lying almost exactly on the border between Italy and Austria. Both countries wanted the Iceman, as he was soon called. For some time the Austrians kept the body, while they argued over it with the Italians, but later it was moved to Italy. It now lies in a special refrigerated room in the South Tyrol Museum in Bolzano.

With modern dating techniques, it was not difficult for technicians to determine the age of the Iceman–about 5,300 years old. He was born in about 3300 B.C. during the Bronze Age in Europe. Understanding how he died was not so easy for scientists, and there is still some disagreement about this.

At first, it was thought that the Iceman was probably a hunter who had died from an accident in the high mountains. More recent evidence, however, tells a different story. Scans of his body showed an arrowhead still stuck in his shoulder. It left only a small hole in his skin, but caused internal damage and bleeding. He almost certainly died from this wound, and not from the wound on his head. He probably had been in some kind of battle. This could have been part of a larger war, or he may have been fighting off bandits (criminals). He may even have been a bandit himself.

By studying his clothes and tools, scientists have already learned a great deal from the Iceman about the times he lived in. We may never know the full story of how he died, but he has given us important clues to the history of those distant times.

C. **Discuss these questions with a partner. Do not look back at the article.**

   1. Did you find the answers to your questions?

   2. What is the passage about?

   3. Where do you think it came from?

   4. Will it be difficult to read? Why?

D. **Read the article carefully. Then, with a partner, retell the events.**

UNIT 1
Scanning and Previewing

TEST 6   Previewing

A. Work with another student. Read the title of the article. Then write three previewing questions on a separate piece of paper.

B. Preview the text quickly and look for the answers to your previewing questions.

Two Languages Better Than One

Parents who come from two different language backgrounds often wonder how they should deal with language. Should they each talk with their children in their own language, or should they choose one and use only that? Similarly, when families move to another country, parents wonder if they should speak to children in their native language or use the local language.

The advice parents get in these situations is not always helpful. They may be told, for example, that children who hear two languages will learn to speak later or will have difficulty at school. This is a common belief among people who have had no experience of bilingualism. In fact, research has shown that the opposite is true: growing up with two languages gives children an advantage.

Recent studies of five and six-year-old children in Canada showed why this is so. The scientists tested two groups for their knowledge of English. One group was made up of monolingual children and the other of bilingual children. The children in both groups knew the same amount of language (vocabulary and grammar). But then the scientists asked different kinds of questions to find out about the children's understanding of language. This was where the groups showed important differences.

One of the questions focused on a sentence that made no sense: "Apples grow on noses." The scientists said it to the children and then asked them if it was a grammatically correct sentence. The monolingual children were confused. They said it was a silly sentence, and could not answer the question about whether it was correct or not. In other words, they could not separate the meaning from the words in the sentence.

The bilingual children, on the other hand, were able to answer the question. They knew that it made no sense, but they also realized that it followed the rules of English grammar. In other words, it was a silly sentence, but you could say it. The bilinguals understood better how language works and how it relates to the world. Children with this kind of knowledge are more likely to move ahead faster in school in all areas involving the use of language.

Being bilingual affects the brain—and learning—in other ways as well. Compared with monolinguals, bilinguals are better able to focus their attention and keep it focused. They are also more skilled at holding two different things in their minds and moving between them. This is the result of all the practice their brain gets sorting out linguistic information and switching between languages. These skills give bilingual children another advantage in school. Not surprisingly, they perform better on average than monolingual children.

But for children to have these advantages, they need to become truly bilingual. A few years of a foreign language in school will not make a difference. Parents who are wondering about language use in the home should keep this in mind. They will be giving their children a great gift by raising them as bilinguals.

C. Discuss these questions with a partner. Do not look back at the article.

1. Did you find answers to your questions?

2. What is the passage about?

3. Where do you think it came from?

4. Will it be difficult to read? Why?

D. Read the article carefully. Then, with a partner, retell the ideas in the passage.

UNIT 1
Focus on Vocabulary

TEST 1

A. Write the letter of the definition for each target word. There is one extra definition.

1. **operation** _____
2. **wealth** _____
3. **charge with** _____
4. **exceed** _____
5. **statement** _____
6. **branch** _____
7. **massive** _____
8. **carry out** _____

a. to state officially that someone might be guilty of a crime
b. something that you say or write officially
c. planned action with a goal
d. part of an organization that deals with one part of its work
e. a large amount of money or possessions
f. a sound, action, or event that gives information
g. to do something that has to be organized and planned
h. to be more than a particular number or amount
i. very large

B. Read each sentence and choose the best definition of the underlined word.

1. The Piper Company, which makes very specialized software, was recently <u>acquired</u> by Microsoft.

   a. started   b. bought   c. closed down

2. Professor Jones is <u>currently</u> involved in a research project with Moscow University.

   a. now   b. often   c. soon

3. The mechanic <u>estimated</u> that the cost of repairs to the car would be over a $1,000.

   a. explained   b. calculated   c. said

4. The deadline for completing the research was <u>extended</u> until the end of the year.

   a. shortened   b. fixed   c. lengthened

5. Maria's personal <u>finances</u> are in bad shape; she needs to learn to control her spending.

   a. money she has   b. money she earns   c. money she spends

6. During the earthquake, several people in the streets were <u>struck</u> by falling bricks.

   a. hit   b. killed   c. hurt

7. The company's economic difficulties were a <u>significant</u> factor in her decision to retire.

   a. small   b. surprising   c. important

8. The company's <u>revenue</u> from sales in China is now several million dollars.

   a. amount earned   b. amount spent   c. amount invested

UNIT 1
Focus on Vocabulary

TEST 2

**Complete the sentences. The first letter is given for each missing word or phrase.
Change the word or phrase to fit the sentence if necessary.**

1. Henricks said in a brief *s*_____ that he would not be running again for senator.

2. The corn fields *e*_____ into the distance as far as we could see.

3. Taxes on cigarettes are an important source of *r*_____ for the government.

4. The town *a*_____ some land near the river for a park.

5. The Shanghai *b*_____ of the Art Workers' Association runs classes in drawing, painting, and graphics.

6. The young woman who was caught by the police was *c*_____ breaking and entering.

7. The police *e*_____ that over a million people attended the concert.

8. A *s*_____ number of students borrow money to pay for college.

9. A new director is working to put the company's *f*_____ in order.

10. His speed *e*_____ the limit by more than 20 miles per hour.

11. The country gets most of its *w*_____ from exporting minerals.

12. The research team was led by Professor Wells, but most of the research was actually *c*_____ by his assistants.

13. During the Navy's rescue *o*_____ two of the pirates were killed, but all of the ship's personnel were unharmed.

14. Ralph Stockton, *c*_____ a reporter for the *Chicago Tribune,* writes about local politics.

15. With the new system, we can store *m*_____ amounts of information.

16. A minibus carrying the high school swimming team was *s*_____ from behind by a truck.

UNIT 2
Making Inferences

TEST 1

Read the conversation and make inferences to answer the questions.

A: Excuse me. Would you mind turning down the music, please?

B: What's that?

A: I said, could you please turn the music down! My whole apartment is rattling!

B: Oh . . .

Is that better?

A: A little better. It *is* after midnight.

B: Oh, come on man, it's still early. It's my birthday, you know, so I asked a few friends over. You wanna come in?

A: No, no, I'm not the partying type and I've got to get up early tomorrow.

B: But it's Sunday tomorrow. What do you have to get up for so early?

A: That's none of your business. The rules say no noise after 11:00 P.M. So if you're going to continue, I'll have to call the police.

B: Don't get so uptight. I get the point. I'll keep it down.

1. Where are these people?
2. What are they talking about?
3. What can you infer about A?
4. What can you infer about B?
5. What do you think will happen next?

UNIT 2
Making Inferences

TEST 2

Read the passage from *Honor Thy Father and Thy Mother,* **a short story by Judith Cernaik, and make inferences to answer the questions.**

In early fall I applied for admission to college. Where should I go but to fabled Ithaca (location of Cornell University)? My mother fought bitterly against it, and when she saw me studying a photograph of my father grinning quizzically[1] at the world from the lap of Ezra Cornell, she tore it up angrily.

"You can't say it's not a great university, just because Papa went there."

"That's not it at all." She was still holding the pieces in her hand. "We can't afford to send you away to college, not as things are now."

"I wouldn't dream of asking you for money. Do you want me to get a job to help support you and Papa? Things aren't that bad, are they?"

"No," she said icily. "I do not expect you to contribute to our support."

Father had apprenticed himself for some months to Grandfather Isadore, and was now installed in the small jewelry shop on the Bowery. His chief customers were his old college friends, Herb and Maxie, and his rich cousin Abe. My mother exerted herself[2] to move out of her cocoon[3]; she picked up a long-lapsed[4] membership in local chapters of Planned Parenthood and the League of Women Voters, so that when Father sent out his new cards, together they were able to draw up a respectable list of names. Whether the names would turn into customers was another question, and I knew that my parents were resigned to a long period of waiting before their modest investment could begin to show returns.

Analyzing my parents' failures, I decided that they had not wanted enough to be rich and successful; otherwise they could not possibly have mismanaged their lives so badly. I was torn between the desire to help them, to change their lives, to present them with some extraordinary gift, and the determination not to repeat their mistakes. I had a superstitious belief in my power to get what I wanted, which events seemed to confirm; after months of dogged[5] studying I won a full college scholarship. My father could barely contain his pride in me, and my mother reluctantly yielded[6] before my triumph and his.

---

[1] grinning quizzically: smiling with a questioning look

[2] exerted herself: made an effort

[3] cocoon: home, comfortable place

[4] long-lapsed: ended long ago

[5] dogged: with purpose and effort

[6] reluctantly yielded: slowly gave in

1. Where are the characters in the story?

2. What can you infer about the narrator?

3. What can you infer about the parents?

4. How does the narrator (I) feel about the father?

5. How does the narrator feel about the mother?

6. What do you think will happen next in the story?

UNIT 2
Making Inferences

TEST 3

Read the passage from *The Hitchhiker*, a short story by Roald Dahl, and make inferences to answer the questions.

"So what do you do?" I asked him.

"Ah," he said slyly. "That'll be tellin', wouldn't it?"

"Is it something you're ashamed[1] of?"

"Ashamed?" he cried. "Me, ashamed of my job? I'm about as proud of it as anybody could be in the entire world!"

"Then why won't you tell me?"

"You writers really is nosy, aren't you?" he said . . .

He took from his pocket a tin of tobacco and a packet of cigarette papers and started to roll a cigarette. I was watching him out of the corner of one eye, and the speed with which he performed this rather difficult operation was incredible. The cigarette was rolled and ready in about five seconds. He ran his tongue along the edge of the paper, stuck it down and popped the cigarette between his lips. Then, as if from nowhere, a lighter appeared in his hand. The lighter flamed. The cigarette was lit. The lighter disappeared. It was altogether a remarkable performance.

"I've never seen anyone roll a cigarette as fast as that," I said.

"Ah," he said, taking a deep suck of smoke. "So you noticed."

"Of course I noticed. It was quite fantastic." He sat back and smiled . . .

"You want to know what makes me able to do it?" he asked?

"Go on then."

"It's because I've got fantastic fingers. These fingers of mine," he said, holding up both hands high in front of him, "are quicker and cleverer than the fingers of the best piano player in the world!"

"Are you a piano player?"

"Don't be daft.[2]" he said. "Do I look like a piano player?"

I glanced at his fingers. They were so beautifully shaped, so slim and long and elegant, they didn't seem to belong to the rest of him at all. They looked more like the fingers of a brain surgeon or a watchmaker . . .

I was taking the car along slowly now . . . We had come onto the main London-Oxford road and were running down the hill toward Denham. Suddenly, my passenger was holding up a black leather belt in his hand.

"Ever seen this before?" he asked. The belt had a brass buckle of unusual design.

"Hey!" I said. "That's mine, isn't it? It is mine! Where did you get it?" He grinned and waved the belt gently from side to side. "Where d'you think I got it?" he said. "Off the top of your trousers, of course." I reached down and felt for my belt. It was gone.

(continued on next page)

"You mean you took it off me while we've been driving along?" I asked flabbergasted.[3]

He nodded, watching me all the time with those little black ratty eyes.

"That's impossible," I said. "You'd have had to undo the buckle and slide the whole thing out through the loops all the way round. I'd have seen you doing it."

" Ah, but you didn't, did you?" he said, "You never even saw me move an inch. And you know why?"

"Yes," I said. "Because you've got fantastic fingers."

"Exactly right!" he cried. "You catch on pretty quick, don't you?" He sat back and sucked away at his home-made cigarette, blowing the smoke out in a thin stream against the windshield.[4] He knew he had impressed me greatly with those tricks, and this made him very happy. "I don't want to be late," he said. "What time is it?"

"There's a clock in front of you," I told him.

"I don't trust car clocks," he said. "What time does your watch say?"

I hitched[5] up my sleeve to look at the watch on my wrist. It wasn't there. I looked at the man. He looked back at me, grinning.

"You've taken that, too," I said. He held out his hand and there was my watch lying in his palm.

"Nice bit of stuff, this," he said. "Superior quality. Eighteen-carat gold. Easy to flog,[6] too. It's never any trouble gettin' rid of quality goods."

"I'd like it back, if you don't mind," I said.

He placed the watch carefully on the leather tray in front of him. "I wouldn't nick[7] anything from you, guv'nor," he said. "You're my pal. You're giving me a lift."

---

[1] ashamed: feeling embarrassed or guilty about something

[2] daft: stupid

[3] flabbergasted: surprised or shocked

[4] windshield: window at the front of a car

[5] hitched: pulled

[6] flog: sell

[7] nick: steal

1. Where are the two people in the story?

2. What can you infer about the narrator?

3. What can you infer about the hitchhiker?

4. What does the narrator (I) think about the hitchhiker?

5. What does the hitchhiker think about the narrator?

6. What do you think will happen next in the story?

UNIT 2
Making Inferences

TEST 4

Read these short articles about places and make inferences to answer the questions.

The Dark Sky of Sark

1   Sark is a small island about 80 miles off the south coast of England. It is only three miles long and a mile and a half wide, and has 40 miles of beautiful coastline. The population is about 600, though that increases in the warmer months with the arrival of summer visitors. But only a certain kind of person is attracted to this island. Certainly not those in search of worldly pleasures such as shopping or night clubs. Sark has no paved roads, no cars, and no public street lighting. Thanks to this, the island has been added to the short list (about a dozen) of Dark Sky Places, chosen by the International Dark-Sky Association. For six months, officials from the association worked with the island community on the levels of light outdoors at night.

Everyone on the island supported the idea of becoming a Dark Sky Place. A lighting management plan was created and many people and businesses changed their lighting to make sure that as little light as possible was directed upwards. Lights have been altered at several hotels, as well as the school and other public buildings. Now hotel and restaurant owners are hoping for an increase in business in the winter months, when the nights are very long—and dark.

a. What kind of person is attracted to Sark?

b. What can you infer about the people who live on the island?

c. What is the International Dark-Sky Association?

d. Why would people want to come to Sark when the nights are long?

The Ancient City of Bagan

2   The ancient city of Bagan in Myanmar (Burma) is sometimes compared with Angkor Wat in Cambodia. It is less-known, but just as spectacular. King Anawrahta was the first to start constructing temples in 1044. Later Burmese kings followed his example. Altogether, at the height of its glory, there were about 5,000 temples in Bagan. Most of them date to the period from the 11th to the 13th century, when it was the capital of the First Burmese Empire. The city was also a center of Buddhist studies, attracting monks (religious men) and students from all over southeastern Asia. But then, in 1287, Kublai Khan arrived with his Mongol army. The Burmese Empire came to an end, though Bagan remained a religious center for several centuries.

In time, many of the temples were destroyed by earthquakes or flooding. Today, several thousand buildings are left, many in ruins. Still, it is a place of extraordinary beauty. Photographs show the temples in the middle of vegetation and reddish dirt paths,

(continued on next page)

with few people, no vehicles, and no modern buildings. The political situation in Myanmar has kept away most foreign visitors. This means that we can only enjoy the site through photographs. But it also means that so far it has remained untouched by the modern age.

a. What kind of place is Angkor Wat in Cambodia?

b. What religion did the Burmese King Anawrahta practice?

c. Did the Mongols destroy the temples when they arrived in Bagan?

d. Why are there so few tourists at Bagan?

UNIT 2
Making Inferences

TEST 5

Read this article and make inferences to answer the questions.

Monkeys in India

In India, there are good monkeys and bad monkeys. The good ones are Hanuman langurs, a kind of monkey that has special religious importance. In the Hindu religion, the monkey god Hanuman and his army helped rescue Sita, the wife of the god Rama, from an evil king. The black faces and paws (feet) of the langurs remind Hindus of the burns that Hanuman suffered during the rescue.

Because of their symbolic importance, langurs are given special treatment by Indians. In some cities, such as Jodphur, several thousand of them regularly come in from the nearby Great Indian Desert. During the dry season, the desert heat is intense and there is little to eat there except insects and desert plants. In the city, however, they are allowed to pick fruit in parks and gardens. People share their picnics with them, and food is left for them at religious sites.

The bad monkeys are the rhesus monkeys, which have become a serious problem in many Indian cities. They spread garbage around the streets when looking for food in trash bags or bins. They tear up and destroy trees and plants to get fruits or vegetables. They leave their own waste everywhere, leading to fear of disease. Furthermore, they are much more aggressive than the langurs, and will sometimes attack people and take food out of their hands.

In recent years, some cities have decided to make use of the intelligence of langurs, and in fact they can be trained to do a job. Their job is simple: to scare away other animals from public spaces, especially rhesus monkeys. For example, when New Delhi hosted the 2010 Commonwealth Games, the city council hired animal experts to train 38 langurs to keep the rhesus monkeys away from the Games sites.

Not all Indians are pleased about having langurs in their cities. Some fear that the langurs might become as much of a problem as the rhesus monkeys. However, this seems unlikely, as the langur population in India is declining. They are protected, not only by the Hindu religion, but also by the government. But not all Indians respect the protective laws. People of other religions kill langurs to use body parts for medicine and farmers kill langurs for stealing from their fields.

1. Why do the langurs come into Jodphur?

2. Why don't the langurs live in Jodphur all the time?

3. How do the langurs compare in size with the rhesus monkeys?

4. Is the rhesus monkey population also declining?

5. Do people from the Hindu religion use body parts of animals for medicine?

UNIT 2
Focus on Vocabulary

TEST 1

A. Write the letter of the definition for each target word. There is one extra definition.

1. **apparently** _____   a. actively

2. **be aware of** _____   b. to make known

3. **issue** (n.) _____   c. evidently

4. **rating** _____   d. to increase

5. **recommend** _____   e. level, class

6. **concern** (n.) _____   f. problem

7. **build up** _____   g. to realize, understand

8. **reveal** _____   h. to suggest

                                        i. worry

B. Read each sentence and choose the best definition of the underlined word.

1. The <u>presence</u> of several foreign students made the discussion more interesting.
   a. production   b. attendance   c. ability

2. In the <u>joint</u> presentation, the Swedish and American researchers summarized their findings.
   a. in several parts   b. officially recognized   c. done together

3. The university has <u>adopted</u> a new approach for increasing security on campus.
   a. begun using   b. agreed on   c. advised about

4. A manager who listens to others will be more <u>effective</u> than one who thinks he or she knows best.
   a. saving time   b. spending less   c. producing results

5. The <u>unemployment</u> rate in Canada has not changed significantly over the past year.
   a. the number of people without a job
   b. the people who do not want to work in a country
   c. the amount of money paid to people without a job

6. It is a <u>myth</u> that women smokers are less likely to get cancer.
   a. common fact   b. story that people believe   c. mystery people fear

7. The <u>vast</u> majority of Americans are in favor of higher taxes for the rich.
   a. small   b. large   c. general

8. No single company has <u>emerged</u> as a leader in the field.
   a. dominated   b. appeared   c. failed

UNIT 2
Focus on Vocabulary

TEST 2

Complete the sentences. The first letter is given for each missing word or phrase. Change the word or phrase to fit the sentence if necessary.

1. High *u*_____ often leads to a drop in consumer spending.

2. The test results *r*_____ students' lack of preparation.

3. As scholarships are limited, we strongly *r*_____ applying as early as possible.

4. After illness, it may take time to *b*_____ strength again.

5. Several serious new issues have *e*_____ in recent meetings.

6. The level of pollution in the city is a cause for *c*_____.

7. The school recently *a*_____ a new cost-cutting strategy.

8. Another *i*_____ that needs to be discussed is transportation: How will students get to and from their classes?

9. The teacher was *a*_____ some noise at the back, but she didn't turn around.

10. Many people believe the *m*_____ that only children can learn foreign languages.

11. The teacher decided that the most *e*_____ response was to pay no attention.

12. The contract was signed in the *p*_____ of a lawyer.

13. The *v*_____ majority of teachers are against the government's changes in the schools.

14. Many couples open a *j*_____ bank account after they get married.

15. Politicians keep a close watch on their approval *r*_____.

16. Students *a*_____ had not understood that the course is required, as very few showed up.

UNIT 3
Understanding Paragraphs

TEST 1

Read each list and cross out the word that does not belong. Then write the topic for the other words.

1. Topic: _____
   president   mayor   governor   prime minister   king   senator

2. Topic: _____
   wheel   handlebar   helmet   pedal   seat   frame

3. Topic: _____
   gloves   pants   shoes   socks   tights   slippers

4. Topic: _____
   Honda   Volvo   Volkswagen   Renault   Porsche   Fiat

5. Topic: _____
   Gruyere   cheddar   Parmesan   Swiss   mozzarella   yogurt

6. Topic: _____
   canoe   rowboat   kayak   speedboat   sailboat   raft

7. Topic: _____
   Paris   Moscow   Amsterdam   Berlin   Rome   Madrid

8. Topic: _____
   sapphire   diamond   ruby   gold   emerald   topaz

UNIT 3
Understanding Paragraphs

TEST 2

Read each list and cross out the word that does not belong. Then write the topic for the other words.

1. Topic: _____

    sink   toilet   towels   shower   bathtub   mirror

2. Topic: _____

    Neptune   Moon   Venus   Earth   Mars   Mercury

3. Topic: _____

    violin   clarinet   mandolin   cello   harp   guitar

4. Topic: _____

    Hawaii   Indonesia   Malaysia   Japan   Samoa   New Zealand

5. Topic: _____

    hiking   sunbathing   running   swimming   walking   aerobics

6. Topic: _____

    snowy   humid   rainy   stormy   breezy   pleasant

7. Topic: _____

    Russia   Canada   Antarctica   Norway   United States   Iceland

8. Topic: _____

    dairy   fruit   meat   seafood   check-out   bakery

UNIT 3
Understanding Paragraphs

TEST 3

A. Read each paragraph and write the topic.

Seashells

1   Seashells serve several purposes for the animals that make them. These animals, called mollusks, have soft bodies with no bones. The shells they make are very hard, and serve as a protection from other animals. Though a few kinds of fish and birds can open or break the shells and eat the mollusks, most cannot. The hard shell also protects mollusks when they are thrown by waves onto rocks on the shore. Moreover, when mollusks are left by the waves on the beach, the shell helps prevent them from drying out. If they remain in the hot sun for too long, they may die anyway. But many survive long enough in their shells for the tide to reach them again.

Topic: _____

2   There are basically two kinds of mollusks that make shells: bivalves and univalves. Bivalves have two shells that are joined together. They include many of the mollusks that are most commonly used in cooking, such as clams and mussels. The bivalves have a kind of "foot," but they usually use it for digging, and not for getting around. Instead, they move through the water by quickly opening and closing the two shells. Univalves, on the other hand, do make use of their "foot" as a foot. They move by sliding with that foot along the ocean bottom. The univalves include many of the more colorful and spectacular shells that can be found in tropical waters. Both bivalves and univalves can close up their shells completely when in danger.

Topic: _____

3   In some tropical places, especially islands, certain species of mollusks are disappearing. There are a number of reasons for this. In some areas, the water has become too polluted. In other areas, the ocean bottom where they live has been dug up and damaged. This happens during fishing for shrimp or other kinds of fish. In tropical areas especially, some mollusks are declining as a result of tourism. Their beautiful forms and colors make them attractive to visitors. Sometimes, the tourists themselves find the shells on beaches; they are also collected by native people and sold to the tourists. To stop this trafficking in seashells, some countries have made laws against taking mollusks out of the country. At airports, the police carefully check each traveler's bags for seashells. If any are found, that person must pay a large fine.

Topic: _____

B. On a separate piece of paper, draw a diagram for each paragraph to show the topic and the supporting facts and ideas.

UNIT 3
Understanding Paragraphs

TEST 4

A. Read each paragraph and write the topic.

Parents and Children

1 A recent European study measured the time parents spent in serious conversation with their children (about opinions or feelings)—only about eight minutes per day on average. In the past, parents and children spent much more time talking seriously. According to the study, there are a number of reasons for this change. One is that more mothers are working and see less of their children during the day. But this is not the only or even the main reason. In general, most people have less time when they are not involved in some planned activity. Then when they are at home, television, video games, and computers take up more and more time and attention. Even during meals—a time when families traditionally talked about their day—watching the television often takes the place of conversation.

Topic: _____

2 Traditionally, babysitting was considered a job for women. In this view, only women knew how to take care of children, so only women worked as babysitters. However, just as the roles of men and women have changed, so have ideas about babysitters. Some parents now look for men to take care of their children. There may be certain advantages to a male babysitter. When the children are boys, it may be good for them to spend time with a man. This may be especially true if the head of the family is a single mother. Male babysitters may also be more willing than female babysitters to play sports and games that require physical activity. The children may have more fun with a man and have more opportunity to get exercise.

Topic: _____

3 In the United States, many parents are not happy with the schools where they live. They may disagree with the way teachers work, or feel that their children will learn better if they are not in a classroom with other children. Some parents want their children to learn things from a certain point of view—often a religious point of view. Whatever their reasons, these parents can choose not to send their children to school and instead, they can do the teaching themselves at home. This is called home schooling. For parents who decide to home school their children, there are guidelines about how to teach and requirements about what the children should learn. Each year, the children must pass tests to show that they are indeed learning. Home schooling is only possible, of course, in families where one or both of the parents have a lot of time to spend with the children.

Topic: _____

B. On a separate piece of paper, draw a diagram for each paragraph to show the topic and the supporting facts and ideas.

UNIT 3
Understanding Paragraphs

TEST 5

A. Read each paragraph and write the topic.

Coffee

1   Is coffee harmful for your health? Though it is sometimes said that coffee is bad for you, doctors generally agree that drinking several cups of coffee a day does no harm. More than that amount could increase your risk of heart disease and cause problems for your stomach. But according to the Scottish Health Study, there are no permanent negative effects from drinking two to three cups a day. Some people may find that even small amounts of coffee can prevent them from sleeping well. But that problem goes away as soon as they stop drinking coffee. The Scottish study found that coffee may actually be good for the blood and the heart. The study also showed that coffee has a positive effect on the brain. After drinking coffee, people can concentrate better.

Topic: _____

2   Places that serve coffee—coffee shops, cafés, bars—also serve a number of important social functions. First of all, they can be a meeting place. People often need to meet outside an office—because they are far from their office or they do not want to be overheard by colleagues. At a coffee shop, they can stop to talk for as long or short a time as they wish. They just need to buy a coffee (or another drink) and perhaps a sandwich or pastry, but not a full meal. A coffee shop can also be a good place for people who work at home and want to get out of the house. They can continue to work on their computers, but see people and hear voices around them and feel less alone. Finally, coffee shops are great places to stop and rest for tourists visiting a city.

Topic: _____

3   Where would you go to learn how to make good coffee and run a good café? To Italy, of course. There are more cafés per person in Italy than in any other country—one for about every 400 Italians. More specifically, you should go to Naples. This city is famous for its excellent coffee. It is also home to a new "Coffee University," where you can learn all you need to know about the business of making and serving coffee. There are lessons on the history and production of coffee and on the business of running a café. The success of a café is not only a matter of business, however. The quality of the coffee is important, of course, and so is speedy service. But success depends above all on the people serving the coffee and whether they can make it an enjoyable experience for the customer. People in Naples are experts at this.

Topic: _____

B. On a separate piece of paper, draw a diagram for each paragraph to show the topic and the supporting facts and ideas.

UNIT 3
Understanding Paragraphs

TEST 6

A. Read each paragraph and write a main idea sentence.

Insects

1   In the historic French Quarter of New Orleans, termites are destroying the buildings. These insects eat wood, and they have long been a problem in old houses made of wood. Now, however, a new kind of termite, the Formosan termite, has arrived from Asia. They are much more destructive than other kinds of termites. The main reason is that they multiply very quickly, especially in hot and humid places like New Orleans. These termites are also extremely tough. To get at wood, they can cut through paved roads, plastic, and even some kinds of metal. Though they arrived in the United States quite recently, they have already caused serious damage and cost about $300 million every year in New Orleans alone. The city is trying to fight these termites, but it is not an easy job. While trying to clean out one old library, for example, workers found 60 to 70 million termites.

Main idea: _____

2   In the eastern United States, the deer population has increased rapidly in recent years, and so has the number of deer ticks, a very small insect. Though they usually attach themselves to deer, they can also be found on other animals or humans. Their bite is not painful, but they have become a problem because they often carry Lyme disease. This is not serious if it is treated early. But people often do not realize they have been bitten by a deer tick and might have caught the disease. Doctors also do not always recognize Lyme disease because it may seem at first like ordinary flu. Untreated Lyme disease can cause heart problems and other serious health issues. Thus, prevention is important. In areas with deer ticks, you should wear long pants, long sleeves, and long socks if you go out into the woods or work in your back yard. Afterwards, you should check carefully for ticks.

Main idea: _____

3   We tend to think of insects as unpleasant, bothersome, or even dangerous. However, scientists have also shown that many kinds of insects have an important role in nature. For example, when bees visit flowers, they help the plants have fruit and reproduce. Other insects break down dead leaves, plants, and trees on the ground. In this way, they make the soil better for growing things. Still other kinds of insects clean up and recycle dead animals and animal waste. And then there are the insects that live on larger animals. For example, human skin, especially on the face, is covered with very small insects called mites. We might not like the idea of mites on our skin, but we do not feel them and they are completely harmless. In fact, scientists believe they probably help keep our skin clean.

Main idea: _____

B. On a separate piece of paper, draw a diagram for each paragraph to show the main idea sentence and the supporting facts and ideas.

UNIT 3
Understanding Paragraphs

TEST 7

A. Read each paragraph and write a main idea sentence.

Farming in China

1   The Chinese government has an enormous challenge in the coming years: feeding the population. Until now, the country has produced 95 percent of the grain (wheat, rice, etc.) eaten by Chinese people. However, that will become more difficult in the future. The population will continue to grow for the next thirty years to about 1.5 billion. At the same time, good farmland is disappearing. All the large cities have expanded enormously out into the countryside, taking over land that once was used for farming. Furthermore, in large areas of northern China, severe long-term water shortages have turned some farmland into desert. To try to meet the food challenge, the government is taking various measures. It is first of all helping farmers increase the productivity of their fields. They are also encouraging farmers to experiment with less traditional crops, such as potatoes.

Main idea: _____

2   In China, farmers are discovering that there are advantages to planting potatoes, compared with traditional grains such as rice or wheat. First of all, potatoes need less water to grow than rice or wheat. Thus, they can be grown in areas of the country where other crops often fail because of lack of rain. Another advantage to the potato is that it is richer in calories and in vitamins and minerals. That is, a field planted with potatoes will provide more food value than one planted with rice or wheat. Furthermore, potatoes are a crop that can be easily combined with other crops. For example, in southern China, farmers can plant potatoes in rice fields during the winter. They get an extra crop (and extra cash) this way, and the potatoes improve the soil for the rice.

Main idea: _____

3   In recent years, organic farming has expanded rapidly in China. Experts expect that it will continue to grow by more than 20 percent in the next few years. One important factor in this expansion is the recent history of food scandals in China. Some of these scandals, such as the one involving baby's milk, have deeply shocked the Chinese. Because of poison that was put in artificial baby's milk, at least six babies died and 300,000 others became ill. Now many Chinese want to know more about where their food comes from and how it is produced. Organic products are very attractive to many Chinese because they are less likely to cause health problems. Another factor in the expansion of organic farming is the country's recent economic growth. Many more Chinese families now have extra income to spend and so they can afford to pay the higher prices asked by organic farmers.

Main idea: _____

B. On a separate piece of paper, draw a diagram for each paragraph to show the main idea sentence and the supporting facts and ideas.

UNIT 3
Understanding Paragraphs

TEST 8

A. Read each paragraph and write a main idea sentence.

Plane Flights: A Danger to Your Health

1   Pilots and flight attendants have long known that jet lag can affect their memory. After long flights, they tend to lose their keys or forget their room numbers in hotels. A scientist named Kwangwok Cho noticed this phenomenon when he had to fly often from Asia to the United States, so he decided to do some research. To better understand the effects of jet lag on the brain, he did lots of brain scans. Half of the scans were of people who had just flown a very long distance and had severe jet lag. He compared them with other scans of people without any jet lag. In the people with jet lag, there were clear signs of damage to some brain cells. In fact, part of the brain had become smaller. This was what caused the difficulties with short-term memory. Now more research is needed to find out if jet lag has any long-term effects.

Main idea: _____

2   For many people, sitting still for a long time is one of the worst things about flying. Research has indeed shown that sitting still is not good for you at all. The blood in your legs cannot flow well when you are sitting down, and you are more likely to get a blood clot in your leg. The clot may cause swelling and pain in the leg because the blood cannot flow past it. Furthermore, if part of a clot breaks off, it can travel to the lung or the brain and cause serious problems, even death. To avoid risk, doctors recommend moving around as much as possible during a flight. You cannot stand up often or walk around continually on a plane, of course. But you can help the blood flow in your legs by doing special exercises at your seat. Many airline companies now include instructions for these exercises in their in-flight magazines.

Main idea: _____

3   In the past decade, flight attendants around the world have noticed a dramatic increase in cases of "air rage." This is the official term for what happens when people become extremely upset or angry on a plane. At times, they become so violent that they are a danger to others on the plane. In this case, the plane will land at the first possible airport and unload the passenger. Studies of air rage point to several possible causes. One is that travel conditions have generally worsened, with more frequent delays and more crowded planes. Airlines have also reduced the amount of seat space per passenger, so that people are more likely to feel stressed and aggressive. Another factor is alcohol. Flight attendants say that very often the people who become violent on planes have had too much to drink, either before the flight or on the plane.

Main idea: _____

B. On a separate piece of paper, draw a diagram for each paragraph to show the main idea sentence and the supporting facts and ideas.

UNIT 3
Understanding Paragraphs

TEST 9

Read each paragraph quickly. Then circle the best ending.

1. Did you know that the music played in a store can make a difference in your shopping? You may not think about the music at all, but it can still influence your decisions. Music that is typical of one country can lead you to buy something from that country. For example, if you hear Italian singing in a wine store, you are more likely to _____.

   a. like French wine   c. leave the store

   b. eat Italian cheese   d. buy Italian wine

2. Jenny Lind was one of the best loved opera singers of the nineteenth century. Born in Sweden, she began her career singing in Stockholm. Soon she was performing in cities around Europe, as well as in the United States. Lind was known as the Swedish Nightingale. The name comes from the fact that the nightingale is a small bird that _____.

   a. rarely sings   c. often sings

   b. sings beautifully   d. sings at night

3. The longest train line in the world is the Russian Trans-Siberian railway, which is 5,770 miles long and connects Moscow with Vladivostok on the Pacific coast. Though it takes six and a half days to make the trip, this is better than trying to drive. There are no highways in much of Russia. In some parts of Siberia, there are no roads at all, except in winter. Then people travel _____.

   a. in boats   c. on the ice

   b. on open water   d. on the train

4. On the Orkney Islands, off the coast of Scotland, there is almost always a lot of wind. People have to lean forward into the wind so they won't be blown over. In fact, everyone on the islands walks around leaning far over into the wind. Orkney natives like to joke about this. They say that one day the wind will suddenly stop and _____.

   a. everyone will fall over   c. everyone will keep walking

   b. it will begin to rain   d. no one will notice

5. Jacques-Yves Cousteau, a Frenchman, was a famous explorer of the oceans. On television and in films, he showed viewers a whole new world under water. He was able to do this partly because of his invention, the Aqua-Lung. This was the first machine that allowed people to breathe underwater. They could go down deep below the surface and _____.

   a. come up for air   c. stay for a long time

   b. close their eyes   d. watch television

UNIT 3
Understanding Paragraphs

TEST 10

Read each paragraph quickly. Then circle the best ending.

1. Amber is a yellow-brown stone used in jewelry. It was formed over millions of years from the resin (a liquid) produced by certain trees. The resin slowly hardened and turned to stone. Sometimes pieces of plants or insects got stuck in the resin as it hardened. These are very valuable to scientists, who can learn a lot from them about the natural world _____.

    a. in jewelry   c. around them

    b. in the past   d. of people

2. Accidents are one of the most common causes of death among children. Most of these accidents happen at home and most can be prevented. Great Britain has been working to prevent accidents in the home. Over the past 15 years, thanks to their prevention program, the number of accidents in Great Britain has _____.

    a. gone down by 47 percent   c. stayed the same

    b. gone up by 4 percent   d. multiplied by three

3. Quite a few words for clothes are different in American and British English. For example, to Americans, a vest is a sleeveless sweater or jacket that goes over your shirt. In England, on the other hand, it's an undershirt. To an American, pants are outerwear, the same as trousers. In England, however, pants are worn under trousers and generally not _____.

    a. enjoyed at all   c. shown in public

    b. bought in stores   d. seen in America

4. Alvar Aalto, an architect from Finland, is well known for the public and private buildings, as well as the furniture and objects, that he designed. Aalto got many of his ideas for designs from the beautiful countryside around him. For example, the idea for the shape of a glass vase came from _____.

    a. reading a book   c. traveling in Italy

    b. speaking to a friend   d. looking at a lake

5. Scientists have discovered that butterflies can tell them about climate change. Some kinds of butterflies are very sensitive to changes in temperature. If the average temperature gets warmer, they move north. If it gets colder, they move south. In California, for example, butterflies are now living farther north than they used to. This is a sign that the climate in California has _____.

    a. cooled down   c. warmed up

    b. not changed   d. gotten drier

UNIT 3
Understanding Paragraphs

TEST 11

Read each paragraph quickly. Then circle the best ending.

1. After the age of about 45 your eyes can change. You may still be able to see things well at a distance, such as road signs when you are driving. But you may have trouble seeing things close to you. You may not be able to read the names of places on a map or the small print on a medicine bottle. At this point, your eye doctor may recommend that you get _____.

   a. reading glasses
   b. driving glasses
   c. sunglasses
   d. designer glasses

2. When the *Titanic* left England on April 14, 1912, everyone thought the ship could never sink. The captain was so sure about this that he was not very careful. He made the ship go faster than usual in an area with many icebergs. This extra speed was a factor in the disaster. If the ship had been going more slowly, it might have been able to _____.

   a. hit the iceberg harder
   b. reach New York sooner
   c. go around the iceberg
   d. sink more slowly

3. In the past twenty years, the high rate of immigration to the United States has brought changes to the schools. More and more of the children come from families whose first language is not English. In two states, Texas and California, there are now more students from non-English-speaking families than from _____.

   a. immigrant families
   b. non-English-speaking families
   c. Spanish-speaking families
   d. English-speaking families

4. Scientists believe that birds developed from certain kinds of dinosaurs. These dinosaurs could not fly at first, though they had front legs that were like wings. Then, about 115 million years ago, they developed feathers on their wings. Scientists think that not long after that they began to fly. This was the beginning of _____.

   a. flight as we know it
   b. dinosaurs as we know them
   c. birds as we know them
   d. history as we know it

5. "An apple a day keeps the doctor away." This old saying used to be very popular with mothers to help persuade their children to eat fruit. Now we know that apples are indeed good for you. Eaten regularly, they can help prevent heart disease and other health problems. In fact, old sayings sometimes _____.

   a. hide the truth
   b. contain some truth
   c. do not make sense
   d. confuse people

UNIT 3
Understanding Paragraphs

TEST 12

Read each paragraph quickly. Then circle the best ending.

1. In the book business, people talk about two kinds of best-sellers. The "blockbuster," by a well-known author, gets a lot of publicity and many copies are sold immediately. The "sleeper," on the other hand, is usually by an unknown author. It does not get much publicity and few copies sell at first. But some people read it, like it, and talk about it. They spread the word to other people, to the media, and to bookstores, and in the end, _____.

   a. only a few copies are sold   c. they buy some copies

   b. tell people not to read it   d. many copies are sold

2. At the beginning of Tolstoy's novel *Anna Karenina,* we learn about the Oblonsky family. Everyone in the family is unhappy for one reason or another. The novel goes on to tell the reader about this situation. Most of Tolstoy's novels focus on life's troubles and tragedies. As he wrote in the first sentence of *Anna Karenina,* "Happy families are all alike; every unhappy family _____."

   a. is also happy in the end   c. used to be happy

   b. is unhappy in its own way   d. is boring to read about

3. Breakfast cereals were first made in the United States by Dr. Joseph Kellogg in the 1890s. As a doctor he thought that the traditional American breakfast—meat, eggs, and toast—was too large and rich. He also knew that people had less time to prepare breakfast than in the past, so he invented corn flakes. They soon became popular in the United States because they were not only inexpensive, but also _____.

   a. heavy and rich   c. quick and light

   b. very expensive   d. traditional

4. Roald Amundsen, a Norwegian, was the first person to reach the South Pole in 1911, just days before Robert Scott, a Scotsman. Amundsen also returned safely to his home base with all his men, while Scott and several of his men died on the way back. One reason for Amundsen's success may have been his clothing; he and his men all wore animal fur, like the native people in Norway. Scott's men, however, had only wool clothing. In the extreme cold of the Antarctic, wool was _____.

   a. not warm enough   c. a good choice

   b. better than fur   d. less expensive

5. Giorgio Casadio, from Ravenna, Italy, got his first driver's license in 1935 at the age of 22. He has been driving ever since. He renewed his license yet again in 2010 at the age of 97. Since he was the oldest person ever to renew a driver's license in Ravenna, he was interviewed for the newspaper. He told the reporter that he hoped to continue his good driving record. In 75 years of driving he had _____.

   a. had many accidents   c. never driven a sports car

   b. always worn glasses   d. never had an accident

UNIT 3
Focus on Vocabulary

TEST 1

A. Write the letter of the definition for each target word. There is one extra definition.

1. **sensitive** _____
2. **side effect** _____
3. **vehicle** _____
4. **consideration** _____
5. **balance** (n.) _____
6. **ahead** _____
7. **reaction** _____
8. **recover** _____

a. an unexpected consequence of taking a drug
b. easily hurt
c. to get better after an illness or injury
d. a change because of something that happens
e. to make something necessary
f. in front of someone or something
g. something such as a car that is used for carrying people or things
h. something to think about
i. the ability to stand or walk without falling

B. Find the word or phrase in each group that is NOT a possible synonym for the target word and cross it out.

1. **occur**	happen	perform	take place	develop
2. **source**	beginning	origin	cause	solution
3. **avoid**	give up	go around	not do	stay away from
4. **conflict**	disagreement	difference	direction	fight
5. **affect**	contact	influence	change	hurt
6. **solid**	firm	hard	stable	standard
7. **measures**	steps	efforts	actions	messages
8. **location**	place	situation	position	distance

UNIT 3
Focus on Vocabulary

TEST 2

**Complete the sentences. The first letter is given for each missing word or phrase.
Change the word or phrase to fit the sentence if necessary.**

1. The structure was held up by a piece of *s*_____ steel.

2. Don't believe what he says. His only *s*_____ of information is the television.

3. One common *s*_____ of the new drug is weight gain.

4. Sergio photographed the mountain from the same *l*_____ at different times of the year.

5. Time is an important factor to take into *c*_____. We will only have 30 minutes.

6. He was not able to get any work done while he was *r*_____ from his operation.

7. Families with small children can take simple *m*_____ to keep their children safer.

8. His first *r*_____ to the news was disbelief. How was it possible?

9. Some people are very *s*_____ to sound and do not like loud noises.

10. Twenty years ago, electricity blackouts were common in the area. This rarely *o*_____ today.

11. The stormy weather *a*_____ transportation and services throughout the region.

12. Only electric *v*_____ are allowed on the streets of Wengen in Switzerland.

13. In Shakespeare's *Romeo and Juliet,* their two families are in *c*_____.

14. To *a*_____ trouble, she told her parents she was staying with a girlfriend.

15. At the post office, there was a man *a*_____ of her with several large packages.

16. Elderly people often have a poor sense of *b*_____ and hurt themselves falling.

UNIT 4
Identifying the Pattern

TEST 1

Read these paragraphs. Write the main idea sentence and the pattern for each one.

Cause/Effect Comparison	Listing Problem/Solution	Sequence

Women in Sports

1   In the early twentieth century, few American women participated in sports. Many sports, especially team sports, were considered too difficult or violent for women. They could only play tennis or golf, or go skiing, ice-skating, or swimming. But they could not take part in competitions, and they could not become professionals. The situation remained much the same until the 1960s, when ideas about women in society began to change. However, change was slow to come in the world of sports. In 1970, many high schools had no competitive sports for girls. Many coed colleges (for men and women) did not even have changing rooms for women at the gyms and swimming pools. Real change became possible finally after a new law was passed in 1972.

Main idea: _____

Pattern: _____

2   The new law was called Title IX (Title Nine). It dramatically changed the way schools and colleges spent government money on sports. Before Title IX, they had spent the money mostly on boys' and men's sports. They had explained this by saying that more boys were interested in sports. But as supporters of Title IX pointed out, this was not a good argument: Girls might be interested, too, if they had the opportunity to participate. After Title IX, schools and colleges had no choice. They had to spend the same amount of money on sports for women and girls as for men and boys. They had to provide an equal amount of space for changing rooms and bathrooms, and buy an equal amount of equipment.

Main idea: _____

Pattern: _____

3   When Title IX was passed, there was much discussion about what the effects would be. Some thought that the government money would be wasted on sports for girls and women because they would not be interested and would not make use of the equipment and rooms. However, after only a few years, it was clear that the money was not wasted. As opportunities to participate grew, so did the interest of girls and women in all kinds of sports. They began to play baseball, basketball, soccer, rugby, hockey, and other competitive team sports. They also began to compete in running, rowing, cycling, and other kinds of races. As more and more girls and women participated and competed, women's athletic performances improved and records were broken.

Main idea: _____

Pattern: _____

4   Now, forty years after Title IX was passed, the popularity of women's sports can be measured in various ways. First, many more girls are now involved in sports—in 2010, about one in three girls participated in sports activities, compared to one in thirty in 1970. Second, there are now many professional women athletes who earn large sums of money (though still much less than men). Like male athletes, some well-known women athletes, such as the tennis players Serena and Venus Williams, are paid by big companies to help design and to promote sports equipment and clothes. Finally, while the first professional women's teams did not attract much attention or sponsors, the crowds at these games have grown and they now attract big crowds. This is especially true for basketball and soccer.

Main idea: _____

Pattern: _____

UNIT 4
Identifying the Pattern

TEST 2

Read these paragraphs. Write the main idea sentence and the pattern for each one.

Cause/Effect	Listing	Sequence
Comparison	Problem/Solution	

The American Civil War

1 In late 1860, six southern states decided that they no longer wanted to be part of the United States. President-elect Abraham Lincoln tried to convince these states not to divide the country, but the southern states went ahead and formed a government, which they called the Confederacy. Lincoln still wanted to find a peaceful solution. To avoid conflict, he ordered most of the Union (United States) soldiers to leave the southern states in March 1861, except for a small group at Fort Sumter in South Carolina. However, the Confederate government wanted complete independence from the Union, especially from the military. To make their point clear to Lincoln, they attacked the soldiers at Fort Sumter on April 12, 1861. At that point, Lincoln had no choice. He had to declare war on the Confederacy.

Main idea: _____

Pattern: _____

2 The four years of civil war that followed brought hardship and tragedy to Americans throughout the country. In those years, new kinds of weapons were invented and armies began to fight in ways that were more deadly than in the past. For these reasons, far more soldiers died during battles than in any earlier wars—in North America or in Europe. Because of the poor medical care, many other soldiers died later from their wounds. The terrible living conditions of the soldiers meant that many thousands more died of disease. Altogether, more than 620,000 people died during the war. It also caused great destruction, especially in the South, where whole cities were burned down and thousands of homes were destroyed. In the states along the border between North and South, families were torn apart, with some members supporting one side and others supporting the other.

Main idea: _____

Pattern: _____

3   In the first year of the Civil War, the Union army lost many soldiers who could have been saved. This fact was noticed by Clara Barton, a schoolteacher and nurse. She was from Massachusetts, but when the war began, she was living in Washington. She saw wounded and sick soldiers returning from some of the early battles, and immediately began to help caring for them. Then she realized that something more needed to be done to improve their situation. During the summer of 1861, she began working to improve the organization of medical care and supplies. She herself often rode in ambulances with wounded soldiers and worked to bring medical care behind the front lines during battles. She became known as the "Angel of the Battlefield." After the war, she helped establish the American chapter of the International Red Cross.

Main idea: _____

Pattern: _____

4   The Civil War finally came to an end on April 9, 1865, when the Confederates surrendered at Appomattox, Virginia. Two great generals were present on that day: Robert E. Lee, commander of the Confederate army and Ulysses S. Grant, commander of the Union army. Though these two leaders were on opposite sides during the war, they were similar in several ways. Both were great commanders who knew how to lead armies. Their style of fighting was very much alike, and so was their refusal to give up. Grant and Lee were both very intelligent, and able to understand a situation quickly. At the end of the war, the two men were both able to turn quickly from war to peace. This was shown by the way they behaved at Appomattox, which helped bring peace to the United States.

Main idea: _____

Pattern: _____

UNIT 4
Identifying the Pattern

TEST 3

Read these paragraphs. Write the pattern for each one.

Cause/Effect	Listing	Sequence
Comparison	Problem/Solution	

Coffee

1   Is coffee harmful for your health? Though it is sometimes said that coffee is bad for you, doctors generally agree that drinking several cups of coffee a day does no harm. More than that amount could increase your risk of heart disease and could cause problems for your stomach. But according to the Scottish Health Study, there are no permanent negative effects from drinking two to three cups a day. Some people may find that even small amounts of coffee can prevent them from sleeping well. But that problem goes away as soon as they stop drinking coffee. The Scottish study found that coffee may actually be good for the blood and the heart. The study also showed that coffee has a positive effect on the brain. After drinking coffee, people can concentrate better.

Pattern: _____

2   Places that serve coffee—coffee shops, cafés, bars—also serve a number of important social functions. First of all, they can be a meeting place. People often need to meet outside an office—because they are far from their office or they do not want to be overheard by colleagues. At a coffee shop, they can stop to talk for as long or short a time as they wish. They just need to buy a coffee (or another drink) and perhaps a sandwich or pastry, but not a full meal. A coffee shop can also be a good place for people who work at home and want to get out of the house. They can continue to work on their computers, but see people and hear voices around them and feel less alone. Finally, coffee shops are great places to stop and rest for tourists visiting a city.

Pattern: _____

3   Where would you go to learn how to make good coffee and run a good café? To Italy, of course. There are more cafés per person in Italy than in any other country—one for about every 400 Italians. More specifically, you should go to Naples. This city is famous for its excellent coffee. It is also home to a new "Coffee University," where you can learn all you need to know about the business of making and serving coffee. There are lessons on the history and production of coffee and on the business of running a café. The success of a café is not only a matter of business, however. The quality of the coffee is important, of course, and so is speedy service. But success depends above all on the people serving the coffee and whether they can make it an enjoyable experience for the customer. People in Naples are experts at this.

Pattern: _____

UNIT 4
Identifying the Pattern

TEST 4

Read these paragraphs. Write the pattern for each one.

Cause/Effect	Listing	Sequence
Comparison	Problem/Solution	

Insects

1   In the historic French Quarter of New Orleans, termites are destroying the buildings. These insects eat wood, and they have long been a problem in old houses made of wood. Now however a new kind of termite, the Formosan termite, has arrived from Asia. They are much more destructive than other kinds of termites. The main reason is that they multiply very quickly, especially in hot and humid places like New Orleans. These termites are also extremely tough. To get at wood, it can cut through paved roads, plastic, and even some kinds of metal. Though they arrived in the United States quite recently, they have already caused serious damage and cost about $300 million every year in New Orleans alone. The city is trying to fight these termites, but it is not an easy job. While trying to clean out one old library, for example, workers found 60 to 70 million termites.

Pattern: _____

2   In the eastern United States, the deer population has increased rapidly in recent years, and so has the number of deer ticks, a very small insect. Though they usually attach themselves to deer, they can also be found on other animals or humans. Their bite is not painful, but they have become a problem because they often carry Lyme disease. This is not serious if it is treated early. But people often do not realize they have been bitten by a deer tick and might have caught the disease. Doctors also do not always recognize Lyme disease because it may seem at first like ordinary flu. Untreated Lyme disease can cause heart problems and other serious health issues. Thus, prevention is important. In areas with deer ticks, you should wear long pants, long sleeves, and long socks if you go out into the woods or work in your back yard. Afterwards, you should check carefully for ticks.

Pattern: _____

3   We tend to think of insects as unpleasant, bothersome, or even dangerous. However, scientists have also shown that many kinds of insects have an important role in nature. For example, when bees visit flowers, they help the plants have fruit and reproduce. Other insects break down dead leaves, plants and trees on the ground. In this way, they make the soil better for growing things. Still other kinds of insects clean up and recycle dead animals and animal waste. And then there are the insects that live on larger animals. For example, human skin, especially on the face, is covered with very small insects called mites. We might not like the idea of mites on our skin, but we do not feel them and they are completely harmless. In fact, scientists believe they probably help keep our skin clean.

Pattern: _____

UNIT 4
Focus on Vocabulary

TEST 1

A. Write the letter of the definition for each target word. There is one extra definition.

1. **actually** _____	a. strong
2. **intense** _____	b. to consider
3. **analyze** _____	c. really, in fact
4. **regard as** _____	d. the way someone or something looks
5. **complex** _____	e. to connect to, reach
6. **appearance** _____	f. one part of a situation
7. **involve** _____	g. complicated, with many parts
8. **access** (v.) _____	h. to examine
	i. to take part

B. Read each sentence and choose the best definition of the underlined word.

1. Thanks to her family, she was able to <u>overcome</u> her health problems and continue with her career.

   a. pay for   b. forget   c. get over

2. He got the <u>impression</u> that they knew the answer, though they pretended that they didn't.

   a. news   b. feeling   c. evidence

3. The number of people employed on farms has <u>declined</u> in recent years.

   a. gone down   b. gone up   c. remained the same

4. The <u>contrasts</u> between the present government and the past government were immediately apparent.

   a. differences   b. similarities   c. connections

5. The professor <u>assumes</u> that the students have a basic knowledge of the events.

   a. understands   b. expects   c. knows

6. The manager made it clear that he had no <u>intention to</u> leave his job.

   a. plan to   b. desire to   c. interest in

7. One <u>limitation</u> of the plan was the lack of clear guidelines.

   a. aspect   b. weakness   c. advantage

8. Lower clouds <u>tend</u> to be thicker, whiter, and brighter than high clouds.

   a. are unlikely   b. are always   c. are likely

UNIT 4
Focus on Vocabulary

TEST 2

**Complete the sentences. The first letter is given for each missing word or phrase.
Change the word or phrase for the sentence if necessary.**

1. Sales of large cars have *d*_____ as the price of gas has gone up.

2. We can safely *a*_____ that the results are correct; now we need to discuss the conclusions.

3. With the new software, it is now easier to *a*_____ the results.

4. Many people are never able to *o*_____ their fear of speaking in public.

5. There are technological *l*_____ to the amount of energy that can be produced with solar and wind power.

6. The train was due at 10:00 P.M., but it didn't *a*_____ arrive until midnight.

7. Some business people will pay a lot to *a*_____ the Internet on planes.

8. Young people *t*_____ to know more about the latest technology.

9. The lawyer *i*_____ in the case is a well-known expert.

10. Yves St. Laurent is *r*_____ one of the great fashion designers of all time.

11. *A*_____ is an important factor in the success of a television news journalist.

12. Though she only saw him once, the great violinist made a strong *i*_____ on her.

13. The *c*_____ between the two groups of students was less than expected.

14. When Ralph tried to get up, he felt an *i*_____ pain in his leg.

15. The university bought the land in 1990 with the *i*_____ of building a new stadium.

16. It will take time to find a solution to a *c*_____ problem like this.

UNIT 5
Reading Longer Passages

TEST 1

A. Read the title and preview the passage quickly.

Hans Christian Andersen

Is there anyone in Europe or America who does not know the story of "The Little Mermaid" or "The Ugly Duckling"? These are perhaps the most famous of Andersen's fairy tales, so famous that we no longer think about the man who wrote them and how he wrote them.

Andersen was born in 1805 in Odense, Denmark, the only son of a shoemaker and a washerwoman. Though the family was very poor, his father took him to the local theater and gave him books to read. The boy was tall, thin, and not very good-looking, but he believed that he was special in some way. When he was eleven, his father died, and soon after, Hans went to work making clothes for a tailor. His mother hoped he would become a tailor, too, but Hans dreamed of a different life. At the age of fourteen, he left home for Copenhagen, hoping to become a singer or actor. That dream did not last long, but after some difficulties, he did find success as a writer.

From the age of twenty-one until his death at seventy, Andersen never stopped writing. His writing took many different forms. His first publication was a poem, which immediately became very popular. He wrote other poems and some became classics in Denmark, though they are not known elsewhere. He also wrote for the theater— thirty-six comedies in all. Some of them were briefly successful, but they were not well liked by the critics. Of the six novels he wrote, only one was a success. Yet another form that Andersen tried was autobiographical, including books about his travels and about his childhood. These sold quite well during his lifetime. Finally, there were the fairy tales, five books in all. Of all these forms of writing, only the fairy tales are still published and read today.

It could be said that Andersen was the inventor of the fairy tale as we know it. In fact, his stories were unlike anything else that he or others had written before. This may be one reason for their popularity at the time. He thought of them as simple stories for children, and was not trying to produce great literature. Thus, he was able to relax and tell the stories as they came to him. Unlike most writing at the time, they were in an informal style that is chatty and direct. Another reason why people liked his tales was their simple appeal as stories. Many were based on old folk tales he had heard as a child, while others were based on his own experiences of poverty and suffering. All of them are full of lively characters and situations—at times humorous, and at times heartbreaking.

In the past fifty years, many of Andersen's stories have been made into films. In some of these, especially those made by Disney, the story has been simplified and the ending has been changed. Andersen might not have approved of this, but he would have been happy to know that, thanks to the movies, his tales have become truly global, loved by children around the world.

B. Read the passage. Circle the overall idea and put a star in the margin beside it. What is the pattern? _____

C. Now go back and mark the important facts and ideas: Circle the main idea and underline the supporting facts and ideas in each paragraph.

D. On a separate piece of paper, make an outline of the passage.

UNIT 5
Reading Longer Passages

TEST 2

A. Read the title and preview this news article quickly.

Electronic Devices Targeted on Subway

The number of people using electronic devices on the New York City subway has increased dramatically in recent years—and so has the number of devices that are stolen in the subway.

In the first seven months of 2011, according to the Police Department, 1,000 people reported thefts of electronic devices, a rise of 17 percent over the first seven months of the year before, when the number was only 787.

Police officials said that the department was working to deal with the problem. More plain-clothes (non-uniformed) officers have been put on trains and in stations to try to identify thieves and stop them. Some criminals have been caught several times, but have returned to the scene soon

afterwards and gone back to their activity.

The Police Department has also distributed brochures and held community meetings to inform subway riders about the risk of theft and how to prevent it.

Many of the thefts occur on weekends or during rush hour. The victims tend to be younger people or professionals, as these are the people who often use their devices in the trains.

The thieves have a simple, but effective technique. They travel on the trains, looking for possible targets: people sitting near the doors who are using their smart phones, iPads, Kindles or other devices. These people often are completely absorbed in what

they are doing and not paying attention to their surroundings or the people around them. When the train arrives in a station, the thief moves closer to the target. Just before the doors close again, he grabs the device, runs into the station and out to the street.

Some New Yorkers seem to be getting the message about prevention of theft. One young student at City College, Jaci Tobin, showed how she keeps her iPad in an inside pocket of her school bag. "I don't use it on the train unless I really have to," she said.

Others assume that it won't happen to them. "I've got to use it," said Paul Frisker, speaking of his iPhone. "It's part of my job. But I keep my eyes open."

B. Read the passage. Circle the overall idea and put a star in the margin beside it. What is the pattern? _____

C. Now go back and mark the important facts and ideas: Circle the main idea (if there is one) and underline the supporting facts and ideas.

D. On a separate piece of paper, make an outline of the passage.

UNIT 5
Reading Longer Passages

TEST 3

A. Read the title and preview this feature article quickly.

Overcoming Jet Lag

The day before a long flight you are very busy finishing up at work and packing for the trip. You rush to the airport, just in time. On the plane, you have a few drinks and stay up late watching the movie, so you hardly sleep at all. When you arrive at your hotel, you are so tired that you take a long nap. Then you can't sleep that evening, and the next day, you don't wake up until the afternoon. You have jet lag.

Most people get jet lag when they travel by plane across time zones. There are three causes, according to Dr. Harold Wickham, professor of psychology at the Coldwell Institute in Montreal. Two of the causes are avoidable. First, people are often very busy before they leave, so they are already tired when they get on the plane. This makes the symptoms of jet lag worse. Second, long-distance travelers often have a few drinks on the plane to relax and pass the time. Though it may make you sleepy, alcohol prevents you from sleeping well, which also makes you more tired.

The third cause of jet lag is something you cannot avoid. Long-distance air travel upsets the clock in your brain that controls sleeping and waking. This clock responds to biological cues within your body, as well as environmental cues, such as the amount of sunlight. Without any environmental cues, the brain tends to set its clock to a slightly longer day—more than 24 hours. This explains why most travelers suffer a little less when they travel towards the west, as the plane is following the sun, creating a longer day. When traveling towards the east, on the other hand, the body must get used to a shorter day, going against its natural tendency.

A number of factors affect the way people react to changing time zones. Those who are "night owls"—that is, they often stay up late at night—are less likely to feel the effects of jet lag. Young people tend to suffer less than older people. Personality also seems to affect reactions: more sociable people have fewer problems than people who are more introverted.

Is there a cure for jet lag? Many companies would like you to believe so and would like you to buy the vitamins or medicines they sell. However, as Dr. Wickham says, there is no proof that any of these are very effective. He recommends a few simple strategies to prevent the worst symptoms and recover more quickly:

- Get plenty of rest and eat healthy meals before a long flight.
- On the plane, set your watch immediately to the time where you will be arriving. Try to eat and sleep according to that time. Do not drink alcohol.
- When you arrive, try to follow a normal routine for that time zone. Try not to sleep during the day, or sleep too late in the morning. Spend time outside during the day.
- Avoid alcohol or sleeping pills, which prevent your biological clock from getting used to the new time.

Unlike some of the medicines for jet lag on the market, Dr. Wickham offers no instant cure. But his recommendations have two important advantages: they will not harm your health in any way and they cost nothing.

B. Read the passage. Circle the overall idea and put a star in the margin beside it. What is the pattern? _____

C. Now go back and mark the important facts and ideas: Circle the main idea and underline the supporting facts and ideas in each paragraph.

D. On a separate piece of paper, make an outline of the passage.

UNIT 5
Reading Longer Passages

TEST 4

A. Read the title and quickly preview this passage from a psychology textbook.

How Do We Form Memories?

If the information in your professor's lecture is to become a permanent memory, it must be processed in three stages: first in *sensory memory,* then in *working memory,* and finally in *long-term memory.* The three stages work like an assembly line[1] to convert a flow of incoming stimuli[2] into meaningful patterns that can be stored and later remembered. This model, originally developed by Richard Atkinson and Richard Shiffrin (1968), is now widely accepted—with some further details and changes.

Sensory memory, the briefest of the three stages, typically holds sights, sounds, smells, tastes, and other sensory impressions for only a fraction of a second. You have experienced a sensory memory as you watched fireworks moving through the sky on the Fourth of July or heard one note after another as you listened to music. These short-lived impressions serve an important function: to maintain incoming sensory information long enough for your brain to select some for possible entry into working memory.

Working memory, the second stage of processing, takes some of the information collected from your senses and connects it with items already in long-term storage. It is this connection we mean when we say, "That rings a bell!" Working memory is built to hold information for only a few seconds, making it a useful buffer[3] for temporarily holding items, such as a phone number you have just looked up. Originally, psychologists called this stage short-term memory (STM) a term still in use (Beardsley, 1997; Goldman-Rakic, 1992). The newer term *working memory* emphasizes new information about short-term memory that has been discovered more recently, since Atkinson and Shiffrin proposed their original model.

It is noteworthy that everything entering consciousness passes into working memory. The opposite is also true: We are conscious of everything that enters working memory. Because of this close relationship, some psychologists have suggested that working memory might actually be the place in the brain where we can locate human consciousness.

Long-term memory (LTM), the final stage of processing, receives information from working memory and can store[4] it for much longer periods—sometimes for the rest of a person's life. Information in long-term memory constitutes our knowledge about the world and holds material as varied as an image of your mother's face, the words to your favorite song, or the facts you studied in your psychology course. Long-term memory holds each person's total knowledge of the world and of the self.

_____

Adapted from *Psychology: Core Concepts, Fifth Edition.* Zimbardo, Philip G., Johnson, Robert L., Weber, Ann L., Pearson/Allyn and Bacon, 2006, p. 268–269.

[1]assembly line: production line in a factory

[2]stimuli: plural of *stimulus,* something that causes a reaction or development

[3]buffer: a place in a computer's memory for keeping information for a short time

[4]store: keep

(continued on next page)

These, then, are the three stages of memory—which this section of the chapter will explore in detail. As you read, you should pay attention to the differences in the ways each stage processes and stores information. With these differences in mind, then, you will begin to discover ways of taking advantage of the characteristics of each stage to enhance your own memory abilities.

B. Read the passage. Circle the overall idea and put a star in the margin beside it. What is the pattern? _____

C. Now go back and mark the important facts and ideas: Circle the main idea and underline the supporting facts and ideas in each paragraph.

D. On a separate piece of paper, make an outline of the passage.

UNIT 5
Reading Longer Passages

TEST 5

A. Read and quickly preview the title of this passage from a sociology textbook.

A Global Analysis of Culture

Cultural Universals

Human beings everywhere are the product of the same evolutionary process, and all of us have the same needs that must be met if we are to survive. Some, such as the need for food and shelter[1], are rooted in biology. Others, such as the need for clothing, complex communication, peaceful coexistence, and aesthetic and spiritual experiences, are basic necessities of social life. Cultures are the means by which people everywhere meet these needs. Because these needs are universal, there are **cultural universals**—practices found in all cultures as the means for meeting the same human needs.

These universals appear in both material and non-material cultures. To meet their need for food, all people have some kind of food-getting technology, such as food gathering, hunting, or farming. To meet their need for shelter, people in all societies build some kind of housing, such as a grass hut, igloo, wooden house, or brick building. To meet their need for complex communication, all societies develop symbols and language. To meet their need for aesthetic and religious experiences, peoples all over the world create art forms— such as music, painting, and literature—and believe in some kind of religion. There are more than 60 other cultural universals, including incest taboos[2], myths, folklore, medicine, cooking, feasting, dancing, and so on . . .

Culture Clash

While cultural universals reflect the *general* means by which all societies meet their common needs, the *specific* content of these means varies from culture to culture. For example, religion is a cultural universal, but its specific content varies from one culture to another, as can be seen in the differences among Christianity, Islam, Judaism, Confucianism, and so on. These religions, along with other values, norms, and languages, constitute the specific cultures of various societies. These cultures can be classified into larger groupings called *cultural domains,* popularly known as *civilizations.* There are, according to Samuel Huntington (1996), about eight cultural domains in the world today (Western, Confucian, Japanese, Islamic, Hindu, Slavic-Orthodox, Latin American, African).

The differences among these cultural domains can be expected to generate most of the conflict around the globe. As Huntington (1996) observes, in the new world emerging from the ashes[3] of the cold war, the dominating source of international conflict will no longer be political or economic but instead cultural. Huntington offers a number of reasons, including the following.

Adapted from *Sociology: A Brief Introduction.* Thio, Alex. Pearson Education., 2005, p. 56–57.

[1]shelter: housing

[2]taboo: when something should be avoided

[3]ashes: gray substance left after a fire

(continued on next page)

First, differences among cultures are real and basic. A common example is the differences in language around the globe. These linguistic differences have for centuries produced the most violent conflicts, as in the form of wars between tribes or nation-states in Africa and Asia.

Second, the world is shrinking[4], increasing interactions between peoples with different cultures. This reinforces awareness of the differences between cultures, such as American and Japanese cultures, and the common characteristics within a culture, such as the Western culture shared by the United States, Canada, and Western Europe. This partly explains why Americans react far more negatively to Japanese or Chinese investment in the United States than to investments from Canada and Western Europe.

Third, economic modernization and social changes are destroying local traditions, which in the past were the source of identity for much of the world. Religion has often moved in to fill the gap, often in the form of fundamentalist religious movements. This may partly explain why terrorist Osama bin Laden and his followers became fanatic Muslims. They blamed Western modernity for destroying their traditional way of life by causing, among other things, their women to be "unveiled and in public places, taking buses, eating in cafés, and working alongside men" (Zakaria, 2001).

_____

[4]shrinking: becoming or seeming smaller

B. Read the passage. Circle the overall idea and put a star in the margin beside it. What is the pattern? _____

C. Now go back and mark the important facts and ideas: Circle the main idea and underline the supporting facts and ideas in each paragraph.

D. On a separate piece of paper, make an outline of the passage.

UNIT 5
Focus on Vocabulary

TEST 1

A. Match each target word to its definition. There is one extra definition.

1. **determine** _____
2. **serve as** _____
3. **purchase** _____
4. **in terms of** _____
5. **in the meantime** _____
6. **function** (v.) _____
7. **means** _____
8. **provide** _____

a. considering
b. method or system that you use to achieve a result
c. to make something available, to give something
d. to buy something
e. to be used as
f. to work in a correct way
g. to find out
h. in relation to
i. in a period of time from now until a future event

B. Read each sentence and choose the best definition of the underlined word.

1. When the economy slows down, people tend to stop buying consumer <u>goods</u> such as refrigerators or cars.
   a. kinds of machines   b. things produced to be sold   c. things found in a house

2. Before you can become an auto mechanic these days, you need <u>specialized</u> training.
   a. for a particular purpose   b. that lasts a long time   c. at a special school

3. My mother had lots of ideas about how to fix things but they were never <u>practical</u>.
   a. doable   b. affordable   c. simple

4. Most of the students improved over the semester, <u>with the exception of</u> Veronica.
   a. as well as   b. not including   c. for example

5. To <u>appreciate</u> some modern music, you need to listen to it several times.
   a. understand   b. perform well   c. hear clearly

6. During the war, many people <u>traded</u> personal possessions such as jewelry for food.
   a. acquired   b. developed   c. exchanged

7. Many Chinese factory workers <u>are willing to</u> live in very basic conditions.
   a. are prepared to   b. might refuse to   c. will have to

8. After 2008, the Canadian economy <u>experienced</u> less unemployment than the American economy.
   a. expanded into   b. experimented with   c. was affected by

UNIT 5
Focus on Vocabulary

TEST 2

Complete the sentences. The first letter is given for each missing word or phrase. Change the word or phrase to fit the sentence if necessary.

1. With a few *e*_____, the local leaders supported the new mayor.

2. With the higher cost of oil and gas, prices also rose for consumer *g*_____, such as televisions and refrigerators.

3. Scientists still do not understand how some parts of the brain *f*_____.

4. The college *e*_____ a period of strong growth during the 1990s.

5. In some developing countries, bicycles are the only *m*_____ of transportation for many people.

6. Many people are *w*_____ to pay more for food that is fresh and free of chemicals.

7. Her experience in Africa taught her to *a*_____ other cultures.

8. For most sports, each country has its own organization that *d*_____ the rules and penalties.

9. Work has started on the new bridge, which will be finished next year. *M*_____, all traffic will continue to use the old bridge.

10. The army plans to *p*_____ new jets that cost millions of dollars.

11. In many professions, *p*_____ experience on the job is part of the student's education.

12. Early explorers in North America *t*_____ with the native Indians.

13. In today's work world, young people need more than general knowledge; they need *s*_____ skills in one area.

14. It is too limiting to talk about climate change simply *i*_____ temperature.

15. Tablecloths originally *s*_____ towels for dinner guests to clean their hands on.

16. It is important to eat fruits and vegetables because they *p*_____ your body with essential vitamins and minerals.

UNIT 6
Skimming

TEST 1

A. Work with another student. Read the title of the article. Talk about it together. What do you think happened?

B. Write your exact starting time. Then look through the passage as <u>quickly</u> as possible to find out what happened.   Starting time: _____

Eight Men Jailed Over Safety Triangles

Eight men were sent to jail on Monday afternoon in western Kentucky because they refused to pay fines. The men had been fined because they had not put reflective orange safety triangles on the back of their buggies (a vehicle pulled by a horse).

The men refused to pay the fines because, they argued, that would be like recognizing the law. Local police had asked them to put the triangles on their buggies two years earlier. The state of Kentucky requires all slow-moving vehicles to display the reflective triangles so that they will be visible by faster-moving cars and trucks.

The men are members of the Older Order Amish sect, a religious group that believes in living simply and rejects almost all aspects of modern living. Members of the sect travel only by foot or by horse-drawn vehicle. Their homes do not have electricity, television, washing machines, or other modern conveniences. Men, women and children wear only old-fashioned, dark-colored clothing. They are not allowed to wear bright-colored clothes or to display anything brightly colored on their vehicles or homes.

On Monday morning, nine men were arrested and brought to Graves County District Court. Judge Deborah Hawkins sentenced eight of the

men to between three and ten days in jail. One of them was later allowed to go home. Local people said that a friend had paid the fine for him because he has a young son who is very ill.

"I don't think it's right to put somebody in jail for practicing their religious beliefs," said Mr. Zook, one of the Amish men. He told journalists that they preferred to go to jail rather than break the rules of their religion.

Randy Haley, the Graves County jailer, told reporters that the men will be released on Thursday, when they have served three days. Because of their religious beliefs, they were given dark-colored suits for jail, rather than the usual orange-colored suits.

According to Haley, they have been no trouble, "They were very nice," he said. "They did anything we asked them to do."

State Senator Ken Winters, from Murray, Kentucky, has become interested in the case. He has asked for an investigation into the laws in other states. In his view, it should be possible to find common ground, protecting the beliefs of the Amish, while at the same time also protecting the safety of people on the roads in Kentucky.

Finishing time: _____

C. Write your finishing time and calculate your reading time: _____

D. Work with your partner. Can you tell what happened? Do not look back at the article.

E. Check your understanding by reading the article again more carefully.

UNIT 6
Skimming

TEST 2

A. Work with another student. Read the title of the book review. What can you tell about the book?

B. Write your exact starting time. Then look through the review as <u>quickly</u> as possible to find the main points.   Starting time: _____

The Last Lecture–by Randy Pausch, with Jeffrey Zaslow

At the center of this unusual book is a lecture that Pausch gave at Carnegie Mellon University, where he was a professor of computer science. The university held a series of lectures in which professors were supposed to imagine that they were dying and wanted to tell students something important about life.

But unlike the others, Pausch did not need to imagine anything. He really was dying. He had pancreatic cancer and doctors had told him that he would only live for another three months.

At the lecture, people wept, but they also laughed. His friends said that Pausch had always had a good sense of humor, and it stayed with him to the end. After the lecture, Jeff Zaslow, a reporter for the *Wall Street Journal,* decided to write about it in the *Journal* and put a short video on the website.

Soon the whole lecture was on YouTube, and millions of people had watched it. The popularity of the video led Pausch to write a book, expanding on the lecture (with Zaslow's help). It has remained for months on bestseller lists in America and has been translated into 18 languages.

With so little time left to live, why did he give the lecture and write the book? His answer is simple: He did it for his three young children. His advice was for them, for when they were older and ready to listen. The video was for them, so they could see him at his best— as a teacher. The book was for them, so they could take something of his into their hands.

Pausch's words seem to have touched people in a very personal way. Many of us have thought about death, or have lost a loved one. Pausch's story is sad—he was only 47—but his words are not gloomy at all. He was remarkably positive and felt that he'd been lucky in his life, as he had managed to actually do many of the things he had dreamed of doing as a child.

And this is his main theme: How to achieve your youthful ambitions, how to get the most out of life. He doesn't talk about religion, but speaks with the simple authority of a man who is looking death in the face and deciding what is really important.

"Never lose the childlike wonder," he advises. "Show gratitude. . . . Don't complain; just work harder. . . . Never give up."

Finishing time: _____

C. Write your finishing time and calculate your reading time: _____

D. Work with your partner. Retell the main points of the review. Did the reviewer have a positive or negative opinion? Do not look back.

E. Check your understanding by reading the review again more carefully. Then discuss these questions with your partner.

1. Would you go to a lecture like the one Pausch gave at Carnegie Mellon? Why or why not?

2. Do you agree with his advice in the last lines? Why or why not?

3. What would you say are the most important things in your life?

4. Would you be interested in reading this book? Explain.

UNIT 6
Skimming

TEST 3

A. Work with another student. Read the title of the article. What is it about? Will it be useful to do research for a report on natural disasters?

B. Write your exact starting time. Then skim the article as <u>quickly</u> as you can to find out what it's about and if it will be useful.   Starting time: _____

Australian Wildfires Worst Ever   (February 12, 2009)

A week after wildfires started in parts of southern Australia, the country is in shock. In the state of Victoria more than 180 people have been killed and thousands are homeless. Police say that the number of victims could rise to 300 by the time authorities have finished searching burned out buildings.

The flames spread over an area of 868,000 acres (360,000 hectares). In the mountainous region less than 50 miles (80 km) north of Melbourne, two historic towns, Kinglake and Marysville, were destroyed almost completely.

According to witnesses, the flames traveled at the speed of a train and burned so hot that car parts melted and buildings disappeared in seconds.

These were not the first wildfires that have taken lives in Australia. Victoria has twice been hit by devastating fires: On "Black Friday" in January 1939, 71 people were killed; and 75 died on "Ash Wednesday" in February 1983.

Experts had warned of the high fire risk this summer, due to the twelve-year dry spell. Furthermore, this summer has been the hottest on record in Australia, with many days of temperatures over 100° F (38° C). Once the fires started, they quickly grew out of control because of the winds blowing in from the nearby desert at up to 60 miles per hour (100 kph).

Adding to the risk was the fact that the forest service had not carried out preventative controlled burning for several years, due to complaints from Melbourne about the resulting smoke. This created a dangerous amount of burnable material on the ground.

In a government report published in 2007, climate scientists predicted that the average number of days with temperatures over 95° F (35° C) would rise from nine to twenty-one by 2050. The fire season would start sooner in the summer, end later, and be more intense. The events of this summer seem to confirm these predictions.

The government of Prime Minister Rudd has promised US$15 million (A$24) in aid to the state of Victoria for rebuilding homes and communities. On top of that, Australians around the country have donated almost US$22 million (A$34).

The government has also said it will review fire-management strategies and reassess advice given to people in fire zones. Many waited too long to leave their homes and were caught in their cars by the fast-moving flames. Others, who stayed in their homes to try to save them, did not survive the intense heat.

Finishing time: _____

C. Write your finishing time and calculate your reading time: _____

D. Work with your partner. Retell the main points of the article. Do not look back.

E. Check your understanding by reading the article again more carefully. Then discuss these questions with your partner.

  1. How serious were the fires?

  2. What were the effects in terms of damage to people and places?

  3. Is there scientific information in the article? If so, underline the sentences with scientific information.

  4. Is there information about people's reactions? Is there information about the causes? If so, make a star in the margin beside information about people's reactions and circle information about the causes.

UNIT 6
Skimming

TEST 4

A. Work with another student. Read the title of the article. What is it about? Will it be useful to do research for a report on natural disasters?

B. Write your exact starting time. Then skim the article as <u>quickly</u> as you can to find out what it's about and if it will be useful.   Starting time: _____

Heat, Smoke Suffocate Moscow   (August 10, 2010)

For almost two weeks, Moscow has been covered by a thick layer of smoke. It comes from 554 wildfires that have burned over 410,000 acres outside the city and across western Russia, causing 52 deaths and destroying more than 3,500 homes.

Since late June, temperatures have broken all records, with thermometers reading over 90°F (35°C) every day. This and a dry spell lasting several years have led to the conditions for the most extensive wildfires in memory.

Many of the fires are burning in peat bogs. Usually wet all summer, the bogs have dried out in the extreme heat. The burning peat has created a thousand-mile cloud of smoke that can be clearly seen in satellite photos.

In Moscow, people have been advised to stay indoors as much as possible, especially children, the elderly, and anyone with respiratory problems. Levels of carbon monoxide have gone up to 6.5 times the acceptable level and other harmful substances have reached up to 9 times of their acceptable levels, according to Russia's health ministry.

A number of people interviewed in the fire zones (who have requested to remain anonymous) have criticized the lack of action by government in the first days of the fires. In recent years, state agencies that were connected with forest protection, fire prevention, and firefighting have been downsized and have received less funding. This is mentioned as a factor in the lack of response and the rapid spread of the fires. Around 160,000 emergency personnel are now battling the fires.

Muscovites are more concerned about the smoke. One mother, Mira Alexandrovica, says that the heat and smoke make her feel as though she were trapped in a burning building. If she had somewhere to go outside the city, she would grab her three children and run. From the windows of her third-floor flat in central Moscow, she sometimes can't see the building on the other side of the street.

Health officials have not released official data on the health consequences of the smoke. The independent Interfax agency quoted an anonymous official as saying that the number of deaths in Moscow in July rose by 30 percent. The agency also mentioned unconfirmed reports of cancer-causing smoke from burning waste, and of radioactive smoke from the area of the 1986 Chernobyl nuclear accident.

With up to a third of Russia's wheat crop destroyed, Prime Minister Putin ordered a stop to exports for Russian wheat for the coming year.

Finishing time: _____

C. Write your finishing time and calculate your reading time: _____

D. Work with your partner. Retell the main point of the article. Do not look back.

E. Check your understanding by reading the article again more carefully. Then discuss these questions with your partner.

1. How do the Russian wildfires compare with those in Australia in terms of damage and deaths?

2. How were the two wildfires different?

3. How were the consequences different?

4. Were there any differences in the way people reacted to the Australian and Russian wildfires? If so, what are they?

5. Which one do you think will have more consequences in the long term? Why?

6. What is similar or different about the causes of the two wildfires?

UNIT 6
Focus on Vocabulary

TEST 1

A. Match each target word to its definition. There is one extra definition.

1. **damage** (v.) _____   a. briefly
2. **release** _____   b. to harm, injure
3. **merely** _____   c. to result from, follow
4. **lead to** _____   d. physical hurt or damage
5. **essential** _____   e. a type of material (solid, liquid, or gas)
6. **substance** _____   f. necessary
7. **arise from** _____   g. only, just
8. **injury** _____   h. to cause, produce
                        i. to let free, let go, give out

B. Read each sentence and choose the best definition of the underlined word.

1. Four very big companies <u>dominate</u> the pig farming industry in the United States.
   a. buy products from   b. do business with   c. have control over

2. In warm weather, the air <u>pressure</u> in tires tends to be a little higher.
   a. force that pushes   b. size or amount   c. thickness

3. The American director of the film seems <u>insensitive to</u> the local culture.
   a. disappointed in   b. unaware of   c. unreasonable

4. The events at the festival <u>ranged from</u> fashion shows to rap performances.
   a. were limited to   b. kept out   c. included

5. Now that we have the data, it needs to be <u>processed</u> and stored.
   a. produced   b. dealt with   c. protected

6. A <u>potential</u> employer will want to know about you as a person, not just as a student.
   a. possible   b. productive   c. open-minded

7. Because of their side effects, these drugs cause more <u>harm</u> than good for some people.
   a. help   b. health   c. trouble

8. The regular practice of yoga can bring <u>relief</u> for some kinds of back pain.
   a. suffering   b. fear   c. comfort

UNIT 6
Focus on Vocabulary

TEST 2

A. Complete the sentences with the word in the box that is a synonym for the underlined word or phrase.

| caused by | hurt | just | notice |
| followed by | important | necessary | possible |

1. If she was <u>merely</u> a girl when her mother died, she was _____ a girl.

2. If the problem <u>arose from</u> her family situation, it was _____ her family situation.

3. If the situation <u>led to</u> more trouble, it was _____ more trouble.

4. If eggs are an <u>essential</u> ingredient in the cake, they are _____.

5. If red food coloring is a <u>potential</u> cause of cancer, it is a _____ cause of cancer.

6. If an animal is <u>insensitive</u> to noise, it does not _____ the noise.

7. If a person <u>dominates</u> a company, she is the most _____ person there.

8. If too much alcohol will <u>damage</u> your liver, it will _____ your liver.

B. Complete the sentences. The first letter is given for each missing word or phrase. Change the word or phrase for the sentence if necessary.

1. It was such a r_____ to finally get started on the exam.

2. A knee i_____ kept Curtis out of the final game of the season.

3. To p_____ your application, we need a photocopy of your passport or other photo ID.

4. The top stays down only if you put a lot of p_____ on it.

5. Though it brought jobs, the new factory did a lot of h_____ to the community.

6. After the tornado passed through town, we went out to look at the d_____.

7. Certain industrial chemicals are very dangerous when r_____ into the environment.

8. Some polluting s_____, such as lead, are no longer added to gasoline.

PART 4: READING FASTER

Evaluation is just as important in this part of the book as in the others. Teachers need to know how students are progressing, and students will take their work on the timed readings more seriously if they know that they will be evaluated in some way.

It is important for the students to know from the outset that they will be evaluated on the basis of their individual progress, not in comparison with anyone else in the class or with an established score or rate. Given appropriate classroom conditions (see the Teacher's Guide), teachers should **expect students to increase their reading rate by at least 10 percent from the beginning of the course,** while maintaining a score of at least six correct answers on the questions.

One way to keep track of students' progress is by looking regularly at the reading rate tables and the comprehension score charts in the Students' Books. This may be enough to get an idea of the general situation in the class and to understand which students are having problems.

For a more accurate idea, teachers can compare the initial rate and score that students recorded for the Practice exercise on page 231 (The Great Lisbon Earthquake) with the rates and scores for the three timed readings included here. These readings are the same length (600 words) as those in the Student Book, so teachers or students can use the Reading Rate Table on page 233 to calculate reading rate.

However, teachers should keep in mind that there is always a margin of error when measuring reading rate because of the subjective factors involved in reading any given text. In fact, reading rate is inevitably influenced by the familiarity of the content and the vocabulary. One text may be about a familiar topic, and so the student reads it quickly. Another text, while ostensibly at the same level, could seem harder because the topic is not familiar, and thus the student may read it more slowly.

Part 4

List of Tests

	Type of Test*	Corresponding Exercise in Student Book
Unit 1		
Test 1	S	Exercise 8
Unit 2		
Test 2	S	Exercise 8
Unit 3		
Test 3	S	Exercise 8

*S = Skill or Strategy   V = Vocabulary

UNIT 1 TEST 1

A. Write your starting time: _____ **Preview and then read the passage.**

Making Magic Today

After the death of Harry Houdini, it seemed that the days of magic shows might be over. Many forms of live entertainment disappeared during the mid-twentieth century, including the vaudeville shows and small traveling circuses where Houdini had started out.

Magic shows did not disappear, however, even if they have changed a lot since Houdini. Now magicians can make use of technology for the lighting, the sound, and the tricks. They can perform in front of millions, thanks to television.

One of the best-known magician today performs under the name of David Copperfield. Born in 1956 in New Jersey to a Jewish family, his real name is David Seth Kotkin. From a very early age, he was attracted to magic as one way to gain acceptance by other children. At the age of 10, he was already well known in his neighborhood. At 12, he became the youngest person ever admitted to the Society of American Magicians. At 16, he was teaching a course called "The Art of Magic" at New York University.

Though he started studying at Fordham University, he left after just three weeks to perform in the musical comedy, *The Magic Man* in Chicago. This was when he started using the name David Copperfield, the name of the main character in the novel by Charles Dickens. The show was enormously successful.

After Chicago, he performed around the country, but his career really took off after his first television show in 1977. He created a show for television every year after that for many years, and for each show he presented a spectacular new trick. Some involved escapes from locks and chains, for example, in Alcatraz prison or at Niagara Falls. In others, he made objects disappear. Sometimes, they were very big objects, such as a jet airplane. One year, he even made the Statue of Liberty disappear.

In 1996, he fulfilled his teenage dream of performing on Broadway, in New York, starring in the popular show *Dreams and Nightmares*. Since then, he has been involved in several movies and in a book about magic. He has also founded a museum of magic, with 80,000 objects from the history of magic. These include Houdini's Metamorphosis Trunk, and the only known recording of Houdini's voice.

These days, Copperfield is one of the best-paid entertainers in the world, earning many millions of dollars every year. In 2006, he used some of this money to buy eleven islands in the Bahamas, which he turned into a special, "magical" vacation place. He has also used his wealth to help others. Project Magic is a program he started that uses magic tricks for therapy in hospitals. Patients have fun learning how to do the tricks. At the same time, the activity helps them regain mental or physical abilities after an illness, operation, or accident.

Copperfield has found that his skills as a magician can also be useful outside the theater or studio. One evening in Florida he was walking down the street after a performance with two young women assistants. Suddenly, a car drove up and four men jumped out. They pointed a gun at one of the women, demanding her money and cell phone, which she gave to them. They did the same with his other assistant. Then it was Copperfield's turn. He pulled out all his pockets, but they were empty—no money or cell phone. The men jumped back into their car and drove off. As soon as the car was out of sight, he had his cell phone in his hand, and he called the police. Ten minutes later, the thieves were arrested. How did he hide his phone? He would not say.

B. Write your finishing time: _____ Then answer the questions.

C. Circle the best answers. Do not look back at the passage.

   1. Which of the following facts is NOT mentioned in the passage?
      a. Copperfield grew up in New Jersey.
      b. He came from a Jewish family.
      c. He was a very good student at school.

   2. When he was a child, doing magic tricks allowed Copperfield to _____.
      a. travel a lot   b. win friends   c. earn money

   3. Copperfield's first big success was in _____
      a. a Broadway show in New York
      b. a television show in New Jersey
      c. a musical show in Chicago

   4. Which of the following kinds of tricks was NOT mentioned in the passage?
      a. moving things from a distance
      b. making objects disappear
      c. escaping from locks and chains

   5. Which of the following can we infer from the passage?
      a. Copperfield is interested in Houdini's tricks.
      b. He has no interest in past magicians.
      c. He likes to read about the history of magic.

   6. Since he became rich, Copperfield has bought _____
      a. a house in Florida   b. a group of islands   c. a jet plane

   7. Who does Project Magic help?
      a. patients in hospitals   b. children at performances   c. guests on his islands

   8. Why didn't the thieves take Copperfield's cell phone?
      a. Because they didn't want it.
      b. Because he didn't have it with him.
      c. Because he made it disappear.

D. Read the passage again. Try to read faster this time. Then look at the questions again and change your answers if necessary.

E. Use the table on page 233 in the Student Book to calculate your reading time: _____

F. Check your answers to the questions with your teacher.

UNIT 2 TEST 2

A. Write your starting time: _____ **Preview and then read the passage.**

Fishing for Lobster in Stonington, Maine (United States)

The work starts very early in the morning. Long before the sun is up, the lobstermen drive down to the harbor in their pickup trucks, jump into their boats, and head out onto the water. All day they pull up lobster traps—200, 300, or even 400 of them.

Each lobsterman marks his traps with colored buoys—floating markers. When he pulls up one of his buoys, there are several traps attached. These must all be emptied. Lobsters that are the right size are put in a box. The laws are very strict in Maine about what lobstermen can keep. Lobsters that are too big or too small are thrown back into the water. Then the traps are set back down on the ocean floor and the lobsterman goes on to the next buoy.

A long day of lobstering is very tiring. Sometimes it can also be dangerous. The coast of Maine is famous for its fog, so thick at times that you can see for only a few feet. Boats used to get lost in the fog or wrecked on the rocks in storms. However, that does not happen very often now, as they are all equipped with radios, GPS, and radar.

Still, accidents can happen. Occasionally, lobstermen are caught by the ropes or traps and pulled over the side of the boats. If someone does not help pull off the ropes and traps, the lobsterman may get stuck underwater and drown. This is one reason why most lobstermen work in pairs. Injuries or death are more likely when a lobsterman is working alone. In any weather, lobstermen always wear heavy boots and gloves. That way, if a rope gets caught on someone's hand or foot, the glove or boot will come off and the man will remain on the boat.

Because it is physically tiring, dangerous, and outdoors, lobstering has traditionally been thought of as a man's job. However, these days there are also a few lobsterwomen in Maine. In any case, men or women, those who go into lobstering all have a love of the sea and of boats. They also like being independent. How many lobsters you catch depends mostly on you—on how well you set your traps and how many you pull up. However, the number of lobsters on the ocean floor can vary a lot. So, too, can the price the lobstermen get for their lobsters.

Most lobstermen own their boats or work for another who does. Boys start off working with older men to learn what they need to know about lobsters, boats, and equipment. They hope to buy their own boat when they have enough experience and money. The first one may be small, old, and made of wood, but their dream is to get a large, modern boat.

In the winter months, lobstermen take their boats out of the water to repaint and repair them. They do not want to have any trouble, with the engine, for example, when they are on the water. All of the traps must be checked, too. A new one costs $60–70, so the old ones are repaired whenever possible.

A lobsterman may be able to bring in $1,000 worth of lobster on a good day in summer. But that is an exception. They usually earn much less, and for several months, nothing at all. Then there are all the expenses: traps, boat repairs, diesel fuel, fish for bait to catch the lobsters, and insurance. At the end of the year, a lobsterman may earn just enough to support his family.

B. Write your finishing time: _____ **Then answer the questions.**

C. Circle the best answers. Do not look back at the passage.

1. How does a lobsterman find his traps in the water?
   a. They have colored buoys attached to them.
   b. He remembers where he put them.
   c. He looks on a map with GPS.

2. Why do lobstermen throw back lobsters that are very small?
   a. Because they are not good to eat.
   b. Because he doesn't get enough money for them.
   c. Because there is a law against keeping them.

3. Which of the following dangers is NOT mentioned in the passage?
   a. getting lost in thick fog
   b. getting wrecked on the rocks
   c. hitting another lobster boat

4. What reason is given for the fact that lobstermen wear heavy gloves and boots?
   a. So lobstermen won't hurt their hands and feet.
   b. So they won't get pulled into the water.
   c. So they won't have cold hands and feet.

5. Lobstermen and women generally love _____.
   a. being independent
   b. danger and excitement
   c. eating lobsters and other seafood

6. Which of the following does NOT affect the amount of money a lobsterman earns?
   a. the number of traps he pulls in a day
   b. the number of lobsters on the ocean floor
   c. the size and shape of the traps

7. Boys who want to be lobstermen start by _____.
   a. studying about lobstering in school
   b. working for someone with a boat
   c. buying a boat and some traps

8. Which of the following can we infer from the passage?
   a. Most lobstermen expect to become rich.
   b. People do not go into lobstering for the money.
   c. Lobstermen come from families with a lot of money.

D. Read the passage again. Try to read faster this time. Then look at the questions again and change your answers if necessary.

E. Use the table on page 233 in the Student Book to calculate your reading time: _____.

F. Check your answers to the questions with your teacher.

UNIT 3 TEST 3

A. Write your starting time: _____ **Preview and then read the passage.**

Food for the Twenty-First Century: Seeds

The island of Spitzbergen in Norway, just 700 miles from the North Pole, is a place where things should be safe from fire, earthquakes, flooding, or hungry people. That is why it was chosen in 2006 by scientists for the Svalbard Global Seed Vault. A seed vault, or bank, is a storage place for the seeds of food crops (plants). In Svalbard, there are thousands of seeds from around the world.

Why are these seeds so special? Because we may need them in the future. These days farmers around the world plant many fewer varieties (kinds) of food crops than they used to. At the beginning of the twentieth century, for example, over a thousand different varieties of rice were grown in the Philippines and there were hundreds of kinds of sweet corn in the United States. Now only about a hundred varieties of rice are planted in the Philippines, and there are just twelve varieties of sweet corn on American farms.

This is one unexpected effect of the Green Revolution, which changed farming in the mid-twentieth century. Farmers switched from old varieties of food crops to new seeds developed by scientists to be more productive. As a consequence, many of the old varieties of food crops have disappeared. This is what concerns Cary Fowler and other scientists. Losing a variety means losing an opportunity to study it and use it to develop even better seeds.

In developing countries, especially in very poor areas, farmers still use the old varieties. For example, in the Andean mountains of Peru and Bolivia, farmers plant hundreds of varieties of potatoes. Most of them do not look like the potatoes grown in developed countries. Some are long and orange, others are round and blue, and still others are bumpy and black. Each one tastes different, and contains different vitamins and minerals. Each one also has different requirements for planting. Some grow well on cold mountainsides, others in warmer, drier places. Furthermore, some are resistant to disease.

This is a very important characteristic for scientists and farmers. Along with reducing crop varieties, the Green Revolution has also led to the spread of diseases and insects that destroy crops. Modern farmers often plant all their fields with just one variety of one crop. If a disease hits the crop, they lose everything. The disease can also spread easily and quickly. This is the case now with stem rust, a disease that is attacking wheat. It has spread from Africa, to the Middle East, and could soon hit farms in Europe and Asia if scientists and farmers do not find a way to stop it.

The Green Revolution made possible a large increase in food production in the twentieth century. However, now food production has slowed down, partly because of the farming methods, which have led to the spread of disease, pollution, and water shortages. Furthermore, because of climate change worldwide, farmers are losing their crops more often to extreme weather conditions. At the same time, the global population is continuing to grow. Farmers and scientists are under a lot of pressure. How can they produce enough food for everyone? There are already millions of people who go hungry every day.

The Svalbard Global Seed Vault will not solve this problem, of course. But at least it may help keep open some opportunities. Scientists and farmers will need to study the seeds, develop better ones, and also help farmers develop better farming methods. Especially in developing countries, this may mean returning to the tradition of planting many different crops—new or old varieties—whatever grows best in local conditions.

B. Write your finishing time: _____ **Then answer the questions.**

C. Circle the best answers. Do not look back at the passage.

1. Why did scientists decide to put a seed bank near the North Pole?
   a. Because it was less expensive there.
   b. Because the scientists lived nearby.
   c. Because it was a safe place for seeds.

2. Which of the following is NOT mentioned in the passage?
   a. The Svalbard seed bank holds seeds from around the world.
   b. The Svalbard seed bank holds many seeds from Norway.
   c. The Svalbard seed bank holds seeds of food crops.

3. The Green Revolution _____.
   a. changed farming around the world
   b. caused political changes
   c. led to scientific discoveries

4. What has happened in farming since the beginning of the twentieth century?
   a. Farmers grow fewer varieties of food crops.
   b. Farmers grow more varieties of food crops.
   c. Farmers have stopped growing food crops.

5. Why are there many different kinds of potatoes in Peru and Bolivia?
   a. Because scientists helped them develop many kinds.
   b. Because farmers could not agree on the best kind.
   c. Because each one is useful in a different way.

6. One effect of planting only one crop on many fields is that _____.
   a. the crop will grow better   b. disease can spread easily   c. farmers can work less

7. Which of the following can we infer from the passage?
   a. The new varieties of food crops are the most productive in all conditions.
   b. The new varieties of food crops are always better than the old ones.
   c. The old varieties of food crops are more productive in some conditions.

8. Which of the following is NOT mentioned as a reason why food production has slowed down?
   a. Climate change is causing more bad weather.
   b. There is less farm land than before.
   c. Plant diseases spread easily these days.

D. Read the passage again. Try to read faster this time. Then look at the questions again and change your answers if necessary.

E. Use the table on page 233 in the Student Book to calculate your reading time: _____

F. Check your answers to the questions with your teacher.

ANSWER KEY

PART 2

UNIT 1

Test 1 *(page 5)*

1. noun
2. verb
3. noun
4. adjective
5. adverb
6. noun

Test 2 *(page 6)*

1. noun; a list showing amounts of money paid, received, etc. and their total
2. noun; one of the areas that some countries, such as the U.S., are divided into
3. noun; the condition that someone or something is in
4. verb; to formally say or write
5. noun; something that you say or write officially and publicly
6. noun; a country or its government

Test 3 *(page 7)*

1. a. peace, calm, prosperity
   b. Stress
2. bears
3. a. close
   b. distant
   c. Diplomatic
   d. inexpensive
4. a. closely
5. a. between
   b. to
   c. with
   d. in . . . to

Test 4 *(page 8)*

1. a. mind
   b. shock
   c. head
   d. affairs
   e. information
   f. opinion
2. a. make
   b. gave
3. a. sorry
   b. owned
4. a. about, on

UNIT 2

Answers will vary.

UNIT 3

Test 1 *(page 14)*

1. noun; the bones of a person's or animal's head
2. adjective; clearly expressed with few words
3. verb; to cut something, usually wood, with a metal tool that has teeth
4. noun; place where stone or sand is taken from the ground
5. verb; to look through something (a magazine, book, store) for no particular purpose
6. adjective; careful to buy only what is necessary

Test 2 *(page 15)*

1. preposition; on, especially referring to a boat
2. verb (phrasal verb); to make something happen
3. verb; to argue about the price of something
4. noun; a small hole that lets liquid out or into something
5. verb; to be good enough or have the right to get something
6. verb; to keep animals in order to produce more

Test 3 *(page 16)*

1. a. noun phrase; signs of getting older or having suffered
   b. noun; period of time you do something
2. a. noun; deep hole in the ground, or a bad situation or place
   b. verb; rejected
   c. verb phrase; to watch or follow what someone is doing

Test 4 *(page 17)*

1. noun; dust, dried earth
2. noun; crop, a plant that farmers grow and sell
3. verb; to plow, to cut and turn over earth

UNIT 4

Test 1 *(page 18)*

1. Prefix: uni-
   Root: form
   Meaning of prefix: one
   Meaning of word: the same size, shape, etc.
2. Prefix: dis-
   Root: courage
   Meaning of prefix: not
   Meaning of word: to persuade someone not to do something
3. Prefix: re-
   Root: live
   Meaning of prefix: again
   Meaning of word: to experience something again
4. Prefix: over-
   Root: work
   Meaning of prefix: too much
   Meaning of word: to work too much
5. Prefix: out-
   Root: live
   Meaning of prefix: more or longer
   Meaning of word: to live longer than someone else
6. Prefix: bi-
   Root: lingual
   Meaning of prefix: two
   Meaning of word: knowing two languages
7. Prefix: pre-
   Root: date
   Meaning of prefix: before, earlier
   Meaning of word: to happen or exist before something else
8. Prefix: mis-
   Root: calculate
   Meaning of prefix: not, badly
   Meaning of word: to calculate badly
9. Prefix: non-
   Root: profit
   Meaning of prefix: without
   Meaning of word: (an organization) using money earned to help people instead of making a profit

Test 2 *(page 19)*

Word	Part of Speech	Root	Part of Speech of Root
1. like(able)	adjective	like	verb
2. power(ful)	adjective	power	noun, verb
3. modern(ization)	noun	modern	adjective
4. forget(ful)(ness)	noun	forget, forgetful	verb, adjective
5. emotion(al)	adjective	emotion	noun
6. prevent(ion)	noun	prevent	verb
7. broad(en)	verb	broad	adjective
8. person(al)(ize)	verb	person, personal	noun, adjective
9. hope(ful)	adjective	hope	noun, verb
10. financial(ly)	adverb	finance, financial	noun/verb, adjective
11. norm(al)(ly)	adverb	norm, normal	noun, adjective
12. sens(itive)	adjective	sense	noun/verb
13. general(ize)	verb	general	adjective
14. weak(ness)	noun	weak	adjective
15. demand(ing)	adjective	demand	noun/verb
16. truth(ful)	adjective	truth	noun
17. thought(less)	adjective	thought	noun/verb (past tense)
18. confident(ly)	adverb	confide, confident	verb, adjective
19. influ(ential)	adjective	influence	noun/verb
20. lead(ing)	adjective	lead	verb

Test 3 *(page 20)*

	Noun	Verb	Adjective	Negative adjective	Adverb
1.	settlement	settle	settled	unsettled	X
2.	sense sensitivity	sense sensitize	sensitive sensible	insensitive	sensitively sensibly
3.	ability disability	enable	able	unable disabled	ably
4.	popularity population	popularize	popular	unpopular	popularly
5.	rest	rest	restful rested	restless	restfully restlessly
6.	influence	influence	influential	uninfluential	X
7.	consideration	consider	considerate considerable	inconsiderate	considerately considerably
8.	value valuables	value	valuable	X*	X
9.	insurance	ensure insure	sure	unsure	surely
10.	development developer	develop	developing developed developmental	undeveloped	developmentally
11.	service servant serving	serve	serviceable	X	X
12.	dependent dependency	depend	dependent dependable	independent undependable	independently

*the meaning of the adjective *invaluable* is *not* the opposite or negative of valuable

Test 4 *(page 21)*

	Noun	Verb	Adjective	Negative adjective	Adverb
1.	formality	formalize	formal	informally	formally
2.	report reporter	report	reported	unreported	reportedly
3.	production	produce	productive	unproductive	productively
4.	weakness	weaken	weak	X	weakly
5.	belief	believe	believable	unbelievable	unbelievably
6.	prediction	predict	predictable	unpredictable	predictably
7.	possibility	X	possible	impossible	possibly
8.	preparation	prepare	prepared	unprepared	X
9.	simplicity	simplify	simple	X	simply
10.	expression	express	expressive express	unexpressive	expressively expressly
11.	substance	substantiate	substantial	insubstantial	substantially
12.	perfection	perfect	perfect	imperfect	perfectly

UNIT 5

More than one answer may be possible in some of the exercises in this unit. Any answer is acceptable if it fits well in the sentence.

Test 1 *(page 22)*

1. up
2. Over
3. Just
4. well
5. farther
6. out
7. way
8. took
9. heart
10. ran

Test 2 *(page 23)*

1. down
2. out
3. on
4. about
5. up
6. up
7. on
8. up

Test 3 *(page 24)*

1. weather
2. story
3. improvement
4. source
5. contact
6. opportunities
7. sight
8. shock

Test 4 *(page 25)*

1. as
2. of
3. over
4. about
5. to
6. with
7. in
8. to

Test 5 *(page 26)*

1. joined
2. raise
3. make
4. took
5. take
6. run
7. have
8. made

Test 6 *(page 27)*

1. raised
2. shows
3. number
4. carry
5. set
6. deal
7. effect
8. deal

Test 7 *(page 28)*

1. serve(d)
2. main
3. focus
4. dramatically
5. recent
6. According
7. run
8. significant

UNIT 6

Test 1 *(page 29)*

1. **Problems with Pensions**

The developed countries [S] today are all facing [V] a similar economic problem: how to pay the pensions of retired people. The problem [S] is [V] basically the result of changes in the population. Thanks to improved health and medical care, more people [S] are living [V] longer. This [S] has increased [V] the amount the government [S] must spend on pensions. At the same time, the birth rate [S] has gone down [V], so there [S] are [V] fewer young people working and paying taxes. Therefore, there [S] has been [V] a significant reduction in revenue for the government. Other economic problems [S] have further reduced [V] spending money for most governments. In many of these countries, young people [S] today wonder [V] what—if any—pension they [S] will receive [V] when they [S] retire [V].

2. Products and Services for Older Customers

In many of the developed countries, the population
  S
is aging. That is, the average age of the population
  V   V
is older than it was twenty years ago. This fact
V   S   V   S
has encouraged many businesses to develop
    V
products and services for older customers.

In the medical industry, for example,

new medicines and technologies
            S

have been developed especially for the health
        V
problems of older people. The tourist industry
                                              S
has also begun to offer services for the elderly,
      V
including special transportation and trips

organized for groups of older people. Finally,

there are many different kinds of products
  S   V
designed for the needs of this part of the

population, including everything from shoes

and shampoos to magazines and furniture.

Test 2 *(page 30)*
The Invasion of Alien Species

In many parts of the world, alien species are
damaging the environment. An alien species is a
plant or animal that has moved from its original
home to a new area. Though some alien species may
not cause any problems, others find perfect growing
conditions and have no natural enemies, and so
they grow and multiply without limit. Over time—
sometimes decades, sometimes a few years—the
new species takes the place of the native plants or
animals. This can lead to dramatic changes in the
natural landscape and various kinds of problems.

In some cases, people have purposely
introduced the new species, unaware of possible
future consequences. In 1876, for example, the
Japanese government brought some Asian kudzu
vine to show Americans in Philadelphia at the
Centennial Exposition. Planted in gardens, this
extremely fast-growing vine, soon got out of
control. Since then, it has destroyed gardens, parks,
trees, and forests all over the southern United States.

On the other hand, many alien species
have been introduced accidentally, as a side
effect of international trade. The Asian tiger
mosquito, for example, probably traveled to
Europe by ship in car tires filled with water. It
has now largely replaced the common European
mosquito in much of Italy, Spain, Greece, and
southern France. Though the tiger mosquito has
not so far caused disease in humans, it is very
aggressive and the bites are unpleasant.

Another accidentally introduced species
is the zebra mussel in the Great Lakes of North
America. This small shellfish may have come over
from Russia on a cargo ship. In just a few years,
zebra mussels have spread through the lakes and
into many important rivers. They form enormous
masses, covering lake and river bottoms. Those
masses take away food and oxygen from the native
shellfish and fish. They also cut off water supplies
for power stations and water treatment centers.
Altogether, according to government officials, the
mussels have caused many millions of dollars'
worth of damage.

These days, scientists and governments are
very aware of the possible negative consequences
of introducing new species. Consequently, many
countries, such as the United States, have strict
rules about importing plants and animals. The
Japanese government would never be allowed
to bring in the kudzu vine today. However, as
long as international trade continues, the risk of
accidental introductions will also continue.

Test 3 *(page 31)*
Ravens: Intelligent Birds

The raven is a large, black bird found in

many areas of the world. It lives in all kinds of
                       S
climates, from the arctic cold of Greenland to

the desert heat of North Africa. This wide range

is possible because ravens are very adaptable.

They eat almost anything, including fruit, seeds,
  S
grains, insects, eggs, small animals and birds,

and leftover food in garbage dumps.

In many cultures, people have included

ravens in their stories and beliefs. Sometimes
            P
these birds are a symbol of death or evil. In

medieval Sweden, for example, ravens were the

ghosts of murdered people. In Denmark, an old

story tells about ravens eating the king's heart

and gaining terrible powers. In other cultures,

however, ravens are seen more positively, as in

some native American cultures, where the god

of creation is a raven.

What has impressed people about ravens in so many different cultures is <u>their</u> intelligence.
_S
Scientists have also been impressed and studies have confirmed that <u>they</u> are among the most
_S
intelligent species of birds. Many people have discovered this accidentally. A man who was hiking in the woods in Canada, for example, left <u>his</u> knapsack for a few minutes while <u>he</u> went to
_S   _S
get wood for a fire. When <u>he</u> came back, <u>he</u>
_S   _S
found the knapsack open, and <u>his</u> sunglasses,
_P
gloves, and other things on the ground. Nearby, a raven was finishing off <u>his</u> sandwich and two
_P
chocolate bars. In order to get the food, the raven had managed to open three zippers.

Along with intelligence, ravens are also known for <u>their</u> ability to work together toward
_P
a goal. This was demonstrated by a pair of ravens in Canada who had developed an effective system for stealing a meal from a dog on a chain. After the dog's owner brought <u>its</u>
_P
dinner, one of the ravens landed not far from the dog and began flapping <u>its</u> wings and making
_P
loud noises. The dog forgot about <u>its</u> dinner and
_P
ran to get the raven. But the raven had carefully calculated the distance and was just out of reach. While the dog barked and pulled at the chain, the second raven flew down behind <u>it</u> and began
_O
eating the dog's dinner. After a few minutes, the two ravens changed places. Once <u>they</u> had both
_S
eaten, <u>they</u> flew away.
_S

Ravens usually make use of <u>their</u>
_P
intelligence to get food, but <u>they</u> are capable of
_S
solving other kinds of problems, too. In the Canadian Yukon, where winters can be extremely cold, some ravens made use of modern technology to survive the climate. The street lights there have light sensors that tell the lights to turn on when <u>it</u> is dark. Normally, the
_S
lights are off during the day, but the ravens discovered that if <u>they</u> sat on the lights and
_S
covered <u>them</u> with <u>their</u> wings, the lights would
_O   _P
turn on. Then the heat from the lights would warm <u>them</u> up.
_O

Test 4 *(page 33)*
The Invasion of Alien Species

In many parts of the world, alien species are damaging the environment. An alien species is a plant or animal that has moved from its original home to a new area. Though some alien species may not cause any problems, others find perfect growing conditions and have no natural enemies, and so they grow and multiply without limit. Over time—sometimes decades, sometimes a few years—(the new species takes) (the place of the native plants or animals. This can lead to dramatic changes in the natural landscape and various kinds of problems.

In some cases, people have purposely introduced the new species, unaware of possible future consequences. In 1876, for example, the Japanese government brought some (Asian kudzu vine) to show Americans in Philadelphia at the Centennial Exposition. Planted in gardens, <u>this</u> extremely fast-growing vine soon got out of control. Since then it has destroyed gardens, parks, trees, and forests all over the southern United States.

On the other hand, many alien species have been introduced accidentally, as a side effect of international trade. The Asian tiger mosquito, for example, probably traveled to Europe by ship in car tires filled with water. It has now largely replaced the common European mosquito in much of Italy, Spain, Greece, and southern France. Though the tiger mosquito has not so far caused disease in humans, it is very aggressive and the bites are unpleasant.

Another accidentally introduced species is the (zebra mussel) in the Great Lakes of North America. This small shellfish may have come over from Russia on a cargo ship. In just a few years, zebra mussels have spread through the lakes and into many important rivers. They form enormous masses, covering lake and river bottoms. Those masses take away food and oxygen from the native shellfish and fish. They also cut off water supplies for power stations and water treatment centers. Altogether, according to government officials, the mussels have caused many millions of dollars' worth of damage.

These days, scientists and governments are very aware of the possible negative consequences of introducing new species. In fact, many countries, such as the United States, have strict rules about importing plants and animals. The Japanese government would not be allowed now to bring in the kudzu vine today. However, as long as international trade continues, the risk of accidental introductions will also continue.

Test 5 *(page 34)*
Chimpanzee Behavior

A band, or group, of chimpanzees which usually contains 6 to 10 members, exists as part of a larger community of bands. These bands the size of which may depend on the food available, may exchange members, join together, or divide up. Some bands are made up of young adult males, others of mothers and young chimpanzees. Membership in the bands is not fixed permanently, and individual chimpanzees come and go freely within the larger community.

Chimpanzees spend most of their lives in trees where they sleep and find the fruits that are their main source of food. They also find some food on the ground—leaves, roots and other vegetable matter, as well as insects and, occasionally, small animals. But they rarely go far from a tree that they can climb to safety if they need to.

The long arms of the chimpanzee are good for swinging through trees, which is one way they get around the forest. However, they can also travel on the ground. Normally when they walk, they use both feet and "arms." They can also walk using only their legs, but just for short distances when they are carrying something in their hands. Chimpanzees are not able to swim and have no way of crossing large bodies of water.

When male chimpanzees are excited, they often stand on their legs and make loud noises. They may also throw things or attack, but this is less common. Female chimpanzees have a new baby every two or three years. The young chimpanzees who stay close to their mothers for a number of years, are full size at about 12 years old. They spend more and more time with other young members of their band, and usually move to another band when they are adults.

Test 6 (page 35)
White Water Rafting

People who are looking for outdoor adventure often go to <u>Maine</u>. <u>This state</u> in the <u>northeastern United States</u> contains large areas of wilderness and many rivers suitable for white water (rafting).

On a (rafting trip), you travel down a river on a flat, rubber boat. In the past, (this sport) was practiced only in the western states, but now several outdoor travel companies offer weekend rafting trips in Maine. They provide guide service, equipment— including the rafts—and even food, and they welcome people who have no experience at all. Thus, city residents, too, can get a taste of the wilderness. All they need to bring with them is a desire for adventure.

"<u>White water</u>" is the <u>water of a river</u> when it moves very fast over rocks. <u>These areas</u> are the most exciting for rafters—and also the most dangerous. Rafting guides must always be looking out for white water and (rafters) must be ready to swim because the raft can tip over. For that reason, (people on rafts) must always wear special life vests that will keep them afloat.

Since these rafting trips are always downriver, rafters can relax and enjoy the scenery when the river is calm. There are deep, dark forests of evergreen trees, lovely open meadows with blueberries, and high mountains, too. However, if the river becomes rough, the rafters must pay more attention. Guiding the raft in rocky areas requires some skill. Strength, too, is required for the very rocky parts of a river that are impassible with a raft. Then everyone has to get out, and the rafts and all the equipment have to be carried to a smoother part of the river.

PART 3
UNIT 1

Test 1 (page 38)
1. about 1,211,500
2. Dan Boylan
3. less than 8,000
4. Japanese, Chinese, Filipinos, and people from South Pacific islands
5. native Hawaiian or part Hawaiians
6. 80 percent

Test 2 (page 40)
1. 127°F (−88°C)
2. 8,000 feet (2,438 meters)
3. 10,000 feet (3,050 meters)
4. polar bears, reindeer, foxes, mice, lemmings
5. mosses, lichens, and algae
6. about 30 degrees colder

Test 3 (page 42)
a. 18   d. 7
b. 7   e. 9
c. 5

Test 4 (page 44)
a. 7   d. 4
b. 7   e. 11
c. 5

Tests 5, 6 (page 46–48)
Answers will vary.

UNIT 1 Focus on Vocabulary
Test 1 (page 49)
A.
1. c   5. b
2. e   6. d
3. a   7. i
4. h   8. g

B.

1. b	5. a
2. a	6. a
3. b	7. c
4. c	8. a

Test 2 *(page 50)*

1. statement	9. finances
2. extended	10. exceeded
3. revenue	11. wealth
4. acquired	12. carried out
5. branch	13. operation
6. charged with	14. currently
7. estimated	15. massive
8. significant	16. struck

UNIT 2

Test 1 *(page 51)*

1. In an apartment building at the door of B's apartment
2. The loud music coming from B's apartment
3. A is probably middle-aged or older
4. B is probably young, maybe a student
5. Answers will vary.

Test 2 *(page 52)*

1. At the home of the narrator
2. The narrator is probably a good student and wants to attend the same college his/her father attended. The narrator is also an independent person who believes in supporting oneself in the world. From the context, the narrator could be male or female, and is probably in high school.
3. The narrator's father came perhaps from a family with money. He attended Cornell University and seems to have had a good time and made good friends there. Since then he has not been successful, has made mistakes (possibly lost money), and has recently had to start a new job working for his father or father-in-law. The mother used to be more active socially, and used to belong to organizations, but stopped going out and doing things. There appears to be some tension between the parents, particularly about the father's past at Cornell. But they seem to be working together to try to solve their financial difficulties.
4. The narrator has mixed feelings: S/He seems to admire some things about his/her father, such as the fact that he went to Cornell, but does not understand or sympathize with his failures.

5. The narrator seems to have fewer positive feelings towards the mother, and partly blames her for the parents' financial difficulties. The narrator clearly sees that the mother is less than enthusiastic about the narrator going to Cornell. There appears to be some tension, particularly about the father's past at Cornell, but the parents seem to be working together to try to solve their financial difficulties.
6. Answers will vary.

Test 3 *(page 53)*

1. On a road in England, in the car that the narrator is driving
2. The narrator is a writer and he's probably not poor, as he has a nice gold watch.
3. He's probably a professional thief who specializes in picking people's pockets.
4. The narrator finds him entertaining and funny, but he is also shocked and a bit worried about what he might do next.
5. The hitchhiker seems to appreciate the fact that the narrator is giving him a ride, but he enjoys shocking the narrator and making fun of him.
6. Answers will vary.

Test 4 *(page 55)*

1. a. People who enjoy places that are wild and beautiful, who like walking or cycling.
   b. They appreciate the natural beauty of the island and do not want to destroy that. They like to live a quiet life and can do without cars.
   c. It is an organization that works to reduce the amount of light directed up to the sky.
   d. Because then they can have a better look at the night sky
2. a. It's a place in Cambodia with ancient buildings, possibly temples.
   b. Buddhism
   c. Apparently not because they continued to be used for several centuries.
   d. Because of the political situation

Test 5 *(page 57)*

1. To eat fruit and other food that they find or that people give them
2. Probably because they prefer the wild desert when it is not too hot and there is enough food
3. The langurs must be bigger than the rhesus monkeys, or they wouldn't be able to scare them away.
4. Apparently not. If the population were declining, they wouldn't be such a problem.
5. It seems unlikely from the way they respect and protect the langurs.

UNIT 2 Focus on Vocabulary

Test 1 (page 58)

A.

1. c   5. h
2. g   6. i
3. f   7. d
4. e   8. b

B.

1. b   5. a
2. c   6. b
3. a   7. b
4. c   8. b

Test 2 (page 59)

1. unemployment   9. aware of
2. revealed   10. myth
3. recommend   11. effective
4. build up   12. presence
5. emerged   13. vast
6. concern   14. joint
7. adopted   15. rating
8. issue   16. apparently

UNIT 3

Test 1 (page 60)

1. heads of state or leaders of countries that are usually elected (king)
2. parts of a bicycle (helmet)
3. things you wear on your lower body (gloves)
4. European car makers (Honda)
5. Types of cheese (yogurt)
6. boats without motors (speedboat)
7. cities in the European Union (Moscow)
8. precious stones (gold)

Test 2 (page 61)

1. fixtures in a bathroom (towels)
2. planets in the solar system (moon)
3. stringed instruments (clarinet)
4. island nations in the Pacific Ocean (Hawaii)
5. activities for exercise (sunbathing)
6. weather conditions (pleasant)
7. countries that include some Arctic land (Antarctica)
8. areas in a supermarket with different kinds of food (check-out)

Test 3 (page 62)

1. The purposes of seashells for the animals that make them
2. The two kinds of mollusks
3. Reasons why some mollusks are disappearing

Test 4 (page 63)

1. Reasons why parents spend less time talking with their children today
2. The advantages of male babysitters
3. Home schooling in the United States

Test 5 (page 64)

1. The effects of coffee on health
2. The social functions of places that serve coffee
3. Why Naples is the place to go to learn about coffeemaking

Test 6 (page 65)

1. A new kind of termite from Asia is destroying buildings in New Orleans.
2. Deer ticks are causing Lyme disease in the eastern United States.
3. Scientists have shown that many insects have an important role in nature.

Test 7 (page 66)

1. Feeding the population will be an enormous challenge for the Chinese government.
2. For Chinese farmers, there are advantages to planting potatoes, compared with traditional grains.
3. Several factors have helped organic farming expand in China.

Test 8 (page 67)

1. Studies show that jet lag affects short-term memory.
2. Sitting still on long plane flights can cause serious health problems.
3. There are several reasons why air rage is a problem these days.

Test 9 (page 68)
1. d   4. a
2. b   5. c
3. c

Test 10 (page 69)
1. b   4. d
2. a   5. c
3. c

Test 11 (page 70)
1. a   4. c
2. c   5. b
3. d

Test 12 (page 71)
1. d   4. a
2. b   5. d
3. c

UNIT 3 Focus on Vocabulary

Test 1 (page 72)
A.
1. b   5. i
2. a   6. f
3. g   7. d
4. h   8. c

B.
1. perform   5. contact
2. solution   6. standard
3. give up   7. messages
4. direction   8. distance

Test 2 (page 73)
1. solid   9. sensitive
2. source   10. occurs
3. side effect   11. affected
4. location   12. vehicles
5. consideration   13. conflict
6. recovering   14. avoid
7. measures   15. ahead
8. reaction   16. balance

UNIT 4

Test 1 (page 74)
1. Main idea: From the early twentieth century until 1972, not much changed for women in sports.
   Pattern: sequence
2. Main idea: Title Nine changed the way schools and colleges spent government money on sports.
   Pattern: comparison
3. Main idea: Title Nine had positive effects on women's participation and performance in sports.
   Pattern: cause/effect
4. Main idea: The popularity of women's sports now can be measured in various ways.
   Pattern: listing

Test 2 (page 76)
1. Main idea: The events of 1860 and 1861 forced Lincoln to declare war on the Confederacy.
   Pattern: sequence
2. Main idea: The four years of civil war that followed brought hardship and tragedy to Americans throughout the country
   Pattern: cause/effect, listing
3. Main idea: Clara Barton realized that the Union Army was losing soldiers who could have been saved and she worked to improved their medical care.
   Pattern: problem/solution
4. Main idea: The generals of the two sides of the Civil War were similar in several ways.
   Pattern: comparison

Test 3 (page 78)
1. Cause/Effect
2. Listing
3. Problem/Solution

Test 4 (page 79)
1. Cause/Effect
2. Problem/Solution
3. Listing

UNIT 4 Focus on Vocabulary

Test 1 *(page 80)*

A.

1. c   5. g
2. a   6. d
3. h   7. i
4. b   8. e

B.

1. c   5. b
2. b   6. a
3. a   7. b
4. a   8. c

Test 2 *(page 81)*

1. declined   9. involved
2. assume   10. regarded as
3. analyze   11. Appearance
4. overcome   12. impression
5. limitations   13. contrasts
6. actually   14. intense
7. access   15. intention
8. tend   16. complex

UNIT 5

Note: The answers here are intended to serve as examples of how a reader might underline and outline the passages, but other readers might underline or outline somewhat differently. Teachers should accept students' work if it seems reasonable, is not too inclusive with long parts all underlined, nor too exclusive, leaving out important supporting facts and ideas.

Test 1 *(page 82)*

Hans Christian Andersen

Is there anyone in Europe or America who does not know the story of The Little Mermaid or The Ugly Duckling? These are perhaps the most famous of Andersen's fairy tales, so famous that we no longer think about (the man who wrote them and how he wrote them.)   ✱

(Andersen was born in 1805 in Odense, Denmark,) the only son of a shoemaker and a washerwoman. ✱ Though the family was <u>very poor</u>, his father took him to the <u>local playhouse and gave him books to read</u>. The boy was tall, thin, and not very good-looking, but he <u>believed that he was special in some way</u>. When he was eleven, his father died, and soon after, Hans went to work making clothes for a tailor. His mother hoped he would become a tailor, too, but Hans <u>dreamed of a different life</u>. At the age of fourteen, he left home for <u>Copenhagen, hoping to become a singer or actor</u>. That dream did not last long, but after many difficulties, he <u>did find success as a writer</u>.

From the <u>age of twenty-one</u> until his death at seventy, (Andersen never stopped writing.) (His writing took many different forms.) His first publication was a <u>poem</u>, which immediately became <u>very popular</u>. He wrote other poems and some became classics in Denmark, though they are not known elsewhere. He also wrote for the <u>theater—thirty-six comedies</u> in all. Some of them were <u>briefly successful</u>, but they were not well liked by the critics. Of the <u>six novels</u> he wrote, only one was a success. Yet another form that Andersen tried was autobiographical, including <u>books about his travels and about his childhood</u>. These <u>sold quite well</u> during his lifetime. Finally, there were the <u>fairy tales, five books</u> in all. Of all these forms of writing, <u>only the fairy tales are still published and read today</u>.

It could be said that (Andersen was the inventor of the fairy tale as we know it.) In fact, his stories were unlike anything else that he or others had written before. This may be one reason for their popularity at the time. He thought of them as <u>simple stories for children</u>, and <u>was not trying to produce great literature</u>. Thus, he was able to relax and tell the stories as they came to him. Unlike most writing at the time, they were in an <u>informal style</u> that is chatty and direct. Another reason why people liked his tales was their <u>simple appeal as stories</u>. Many were based on old folk tales he had heard as a child, while others were based on his own experiences of poverty and suffering. All of them are <u>full of lively characters and situations</u>—at times humorous, and at times heartbreaking.

In the past fifty years, many of Andersen's stories have been made into <u>films</u>. In some of these, especially those made by <u>Disney</u>, the story has been simplified and the ending has been changed. Andersen <u>might not have approved of this, but he would have been happy to know that, thanks to the movies, his tales have become truly global</u>, loved by children around the world.

D. Outline: Hans Christian Andersen

Introduction

Overall idea: Some of Andersen's fairy tales are so famous, we do no longer think about the man who wrote them and how he wrote them.

Development
  1. Main idea: Andersen was born very poor but found success as a writer.
     1. born 1805 in Odense, Denmark
     2. family was very poor
     3. went to theater, read books, believed he was special
     4. went to work for a tailor, but dreamed of a different life
     5. left for Copenhagen to be an actor or singer
     6. found success as a writer
  2. Andersen never stopped writing, and his writing took many different forms.
     1. poems—first publication, very popular, others and some became classics
     2. comedies—36, briefly successful
     3. six novels, but only one a success
     4. autobiographical books, sold quite well
     5. fairy tales, only form still published and read today
  3. Andersen was the inventor of the fairy tale as we know it.
     1. simple stories for children, not great literature, so more relaxed
     2. informal style, chatty and direct
     3. simple appeal as stories
     4. fully of lively characters and situations
Conclusion: The Disney movies changed some of Andersen's stories, but made them truly global.

Test 2 *(page 83)*
Electronic Devices Targeted on Subway

*   The number of people using electronic devices on the New York City subway has increased dramatically in recent years—and so has the number of devices that are stolen in the subway.

   In the first seven months of 2011, according to the Police Department, 1,000 people reported thefts of electronic devices, a rise of 17 percent over the first seven months of last year, when the number was only 787.

   Police officials said that the department was working to deal with the problem. More plain-clothes (non-uniformed) officers have been put on trains and in stations to try to identify thieves and stop them. Some criminals have been caught several times, but have returned to the scene soon afterwards and gone back to their activity.

   The Police Department has also distributed brochures and held community meetings to inform subway riders about the risk of theft and how to prevent it.

   Many of the thefts occur on weekends or during rush hour. The victims tend to be

younger people or professionals, as these are the people who often use their devices in the trains.

   The thieves have a simple, but effective technique. They travel on the trains, looking for possible targets: people sitting near the doors who are using their smart phones, iPads, Kindles or other devices. These people often are completely absorbed in what they are doing and not paying attention to their surroundings or the people around them. When the train arrives in a station, the thief moves closer to the target. Just before the doors close again, he grabs the device, runs into the station and out to the street.

   Some New Yorkers seem to be getting the message about prevention of theft. One young student at City College, Jaci Tobin, showed how she keeps her iPad in an inside pocket of her school bag. "I don't use it on the train unless I really have to," she said.

   Others assume that it won't happen to them. "I've got to use it," said Paul Frisker, speaking of his iPhone. "It's part of my job. But I keep my eyes open."

D. Outline: Electronic Devices Targeted on Subway
Introduction
Overall idea: The number of people using electronic devices on the New York City subway has increased dramatically in recent years—and so has the number of devices that are stolen in the subway.

Development
  1. In 2011 thefts have increased 17 percent.
  2. Police working to deal with the problem
     1. more officers on trains to identify and stop thieves
     2. distributed brochures and held meetings to inform people about risk and prevention
  3. Thefts
     1. mostly weekends and rush hour
     2. victims young people or professionals
  4. Thieves' technique
     1. look for people sitting near doors
     2. move closer at station
     3. before doors close, grab device and run away
  5. Reactions of New Yorkers
     1. some more careful, don't use devices on trains
     2. others still use them, but more careful
(No conclusion)

Test 3 *(page 84)*
Overcoming Jet Lag

   The day before a long flight you are very busy finishing up at work and packing for the trip. You rush to the airport, just in time. On the plane, you have a few drinks and stay up late watching the movie, so you hardly sleep at all. When you arrive at your hotel, you are so tired that you take a long nap. Then you can't sleep that evening, and the next day, you don't wake up until the afternoon. You have jet lag. ✱

Most people get jet lag when they travel by plane across time zones. There are three causes, according to Dr. Harold Wickham, professor of psychology at the Coldwell Institute in Montreal. Two of the causes are avoidable. First, people are often very busy before they leave, so they are already tired when they get on the plane. This makes the symptoms of jet lag worse. Second, long-distance travelers often have a few drinks on the plane to relax and pass the time. Though it may make you sleepy, alcohol prevents you from sleeping well, which also makes you more tired.

The third cause of jet lag is something you cannot avoid. Long-distance air travel upsets the clock in your brain that controls sleeping and waking. This clock responds to biological cues within your body, as well as environmental cues, such as the amount of sunlight. Without any environmental cues, the brain tends to set its clock to a slightly longer day—more than 24 hours. This explains why most travelers suffer a little less when they travel towards the west as the plane is following the sun, creating a longer day. When traveling towards the east, on the other hand, the body must get used to a shorter day, going against its natural tendency.

A number of factors affect the way people react to changing time zones. Those who are "night owls"—that is, they often stay up late at night—are less likely to feel the effects of jet lag. Young people tend to suffer less than older people. Personality also seems to affect reactions: more sociable people have fewer problems than people who are more introverted.

Is there a cure for jet lag? Many companies would like you to believe there is—and buy the vitamins or medicines they sell. However, as Dr. Wickham says, there is no proof that any of these are very effective. He recommends a few simple strategies to prevent the worst symptoms and recover more quickly:

• Get plenty of rest and eat healthy meals before a long flight.
• On the plane, set your watch immediately to the time where you will be arriving. Try to eat and sleep according to that time. Do not drink alcohol.
• When you arrive, try to follow a normal routine for that time zone. Try not to sleep during the day, or sleep too late in the morning. Spend time outside during the day.

• Avoid alcohol or sleeping pills, which prevent your biological clock from getting used to the new time.

Unlike some of the medicines for jet lag on the market, Dr. Wickham offers no instant cure. But his recommendations have two important advantages: they will not harm your health in any way and they cost nothing.

D. Outline: Overcoming Jet Lag
Introduction
Overall idea: There are several causes of jet lag and
             some ways to try to prevent it.
Development
  1. Main idea: Two causes of jet lag are avoidable
     (Dr. Harold Wickham)
     1. busy before flight, so tired before getting on plane.
     2. alcohol prevents sleeping well, so more tired.
  2. Main idea: Another cause of jet lag is unavoidable.
     1. biological clock upset by long-distance travel
     2. clock affected by biological and environmental cues
     3. people tend to suffer less traveling west
  3. Main idea: Some factors affect the way people react to changing time zones,
     1. night owls suffer less
     2. younger people less
     3. sociable people less
  4. Main idea: There's no instant cure, but there are some strategies to help prevent jet lag.
     1. medicines and vitamins not effective
     2. Before flight: get rest and eat healthy meals
     3. On the plane: set your clock to new time
     4. When you arrive, follow routine for new time
     5. Avoid alcohol or sleeping pills
Conclusion: The recommendations are not an instant
           cure for jet lag, but they will not hurt
           you and they do not cost anything.

Test 4 *(page 85)*
How Do We Form Memories?
If the information in your professor's lecture is to become a permanent memory, it must be processed in three stages: first in *sensory memory,* then in *working memory,* and finally in *long-term memory.* ✱
The three stages work like an assembly line to convert a flow of incoming stimuli into meaningful patterns that can be stored and later remembered. This model, originally developed by Richard Atkinson and Richard Shiffrin (1968), is now widely accepted—with some further details and changes.

Sensory memory, the briefest of the three stages, typically holds sights, sounds, smells, tastes, and other sensory impressions for only a fraction of a second. You have experienced a sensory memory as you watched fireworks moving through the sky on the Fourth of July or heard one note after another as you listened to music. These short-lived impressions serve an important <u>function: to maintain incoming sensory information long enough for your brain to select some for possible entry into working memory.</u>

<u>Working memory,</u> the <u>second stage</u> of processing, takes some of the information collected from your sense and connects it with items already in long-term storage. (It is this connection we mean when we say, "That rings a bell!") Working memory is built to hold information for <u>only a few seconds,</u> making it a useful buffer for temporarily holding items, such as a phone number you have just looked up. Originally, psychologists <u>called this stage short-term memory</u> (STM) a term still in use (Beardsley, 1997b; Goldman-Rakic, 1992). The newer term *working memory* emphasizes new information about short-term memory that has been discovered more recently, since Atkinson and Shiffrin proposed their original model.

It is noteworthy that <u>everything entering consciousness passes into working memory.</u> The opposite is also true: <u>We are conscious of everything that enters working memory.</u> Because of this close relationship, some psychologists have suggested that working memory might actually be the place in the brain where we can locate human consciousness.

<u>Long-term memory (LTM),</u> the <u>final stage</u> of processing, receives information from working memory and can store it for much longer periods—sometimes for the rest of a person's life. Information in long-term memory constitutes <u>our knowledge about the world</u> and holds material as varied as an image of your mother's face, the words to your favorite song, or the facts you studied in your psychology course. Long-term memory holds each person's total knowledge of the world and of the self.

These, then, are <u>the three stages of memory</u>—which this section of the chapter will explore in detail. As you read, you should pay attention to the <u>differences in the ways each stage processes and stores information.</u> With these differences in mind, then, you will begin to <u>discover ways of taking advantage of the characteristics of each stage to enhance your own memory abilities.</u>

D. Outline: How Do We Form Memories?
Introduction
Overall idea: The three stages of memory work like an assembly line to convert incoming stimuli into meaningful patterns that can be stored and remembered.

Development
1. Main idea: Sensory memory is the first stage
    1. briefest—fraction of a second
       holds sights, sounds, smells, tastes, and other sensory impressions
    2. maintain information long enough for brain to select some for working memory
2. Main idea: Working memory is second stage
    1. takes information from senses and connects it with long-term storage
    2. holds information for only a few seconds
    3. also called short-term memory
    4. close relationship with consciousness
3. Main idea: Long-term memory is the final stage of processing.
    1. receives information from working memory
    2. can store it for much longer periods
    3. holds our knowledge about the world and the self
Conclusion: The three stages of memory have different ways of processing and storing information; you can take advantage of the different characteristics to enhance your memory abilities.

Test 5 *(page 87)*
A Global Analysis of Culture
Cultural Universals
Human beings everywhere are the product of the same evolutionary process, and <u>all of us have the same needs that must be met if we are to survive.</u> Some, such as the <u>need for food and shelter, are rooted in biology.</u> Others, such as the need for clothing, complex communication, peaceful coexistence, and aesthetic and spiritual experiences, are basic necessities of <u>social life. Cultures are the means by which people everywhere meet these needs.</u> Because these needs are universal, there are **cultural universals**—practices found in all cultures as the means for meeting the same human needs. ✻

These universals appear in <u>both material and non-material cultures.</u> To meet their <u>need for food,</u> all people have some kind of <u>food-getting technology,</u> such as food gathering, hunting, or farming. To meet their <u>need for shelter,</u> people in all societies <u>build some kind of housing,</u> such as a grass hut, igloo, wooden house, or brick building. To meet their <u>need for complex communication,</u> all societies develop <u>symbols and language.</u> To meet their <u>need for aesthetic and religious experiences,</u> peoples all over the <u>world create art forms</u>—such as music, painting, and literature—and <u>believe in some kind of religion.</u> There are more than 60 other cultural universals, including incest taboos, myths, folklore, medicine, cooking, feasting, dancing, and so on . . .

Culture Clash

While cultural universals reflect the *general* means by which all societies meet their common needs, the *specific* content of these means varies from culture to culture. For example, religion is a cultural universal, but its specific content varies from one culture to another, as can be seen in the differences among Christianity, Islam, Judaism, Confucianism, and so on. These religions, along with other values, norms, and languages, constitute the specific cultures of various societies. These cultures can be classified into larger groupings called *cultural domains*, popularly known as *civilizations*. There are, according to Samuel Huntington (1996), about eight cultural domains in the world today (Western, Confucian, Japanese, Islamic, Hindu, Slavic-Orthodox, Latin American, African).

The differences among these cultural domains can be expected to generate most of the conflict around the ✳ globe. As Huntington (1996) observes, in the new world emerging from the ashes of the cold war, the dominating source of international conflict will no longer be political or economic but instead cultural. Huntington offers a number of reasons, including the following.

First, differences among cultures are real and basic. A common example is the differences in language around the globe. These linguistic differences have for centuries produced the most violent conflicts, as in the form of wars between tribes or nation-states in Africa and Asia.

Second, the world is shrinking, increasing interactions between peoples with different cultures. This reinforces awareness of the differences between cultures (such as American and Japanese cultures) and the common characteristics within a culture (such as the Western culture shared by the United States, Canada, and Western Europe). This partly explains why Americans react far more negatively to Japanese investment in the United States than to investments from Canada and Western Europe.

Third, economic modernization and social changes are destroying local traditions, which in the past were the source of identity for much of the world. Religion has often moved in to fill the gap, often in the form of fundamentalist religious movements. This may partly explain why terrorist Osama bin Laden and his followers became fanatic Muslims. They blamed Western modernity for destroying their traditional way of life by causing, among other things, their women to be "unveiled and in public places, taking buses, eating in cafes, and working alongside men" (Zakaria, 2001).

D. Outline: A Global Analysis of Culture
(No introduction)

Cultural Universals
Main idea: Cultural universals are the practices found in all cultures as the means for meeting basic human needs.
1. All humans have same basic needs
   1. biological needs: food and shelter
   2. social needs: clothing, communication, peace, aesthetic and spiritual
   3. culture is means by which people meet these needs
2. The universals appear in all cultures
   1. food: food getting technology
   2. shelter: build housing
   3. communication: symbols and language
   4. aesthetic and spiritual: art forms, religion

Culture Clash
Main idea: The specific content varies from culture to culture and this can be expected to lead to conflict.
1. Groupings of religions are called cultural domains, or civilizations.
2. Cultural domain—religion with other values, norms, and languages
3. Samuel Huntington: eight cultural domains in the world today
Main idea: Differences among cultural domains generates conflict around globe.
1. After cold war, source of conflict no longer political or economic, but cultural
2. Differences among cultures are real and basic, for example, language
3. The world shrinking—reinforces awareness of differences, for example, American and Japan
4. Modernization and change destroying local traditions and identity—religion filling the gap

UNIT 5 Focus on Vocabulary

Test 1 *(page 89)*

A.

1. g	5. i
2. e	6. f
3. d	7. b
4. h	8. c

B.

1. b	5. a
2. a	6. c
3. a	7. a
4. b	8. c

Test 2 *(page 90)*

1. exceptions	9. Meanwhile
2. goods	10. purchase
3. function	11. practical
4. experienced	12. traded
5. functions	13. specialized
6. willing	14. in terms of
7. appreciate	15. served as
8. determines	16. provide

UNIT 6

Answers will vary.

UNIT 6 Focus on Vocabulary

Test 1 *(page 98)*

A.

1. b	5. f
2. i	6. e
3. g	7. c
4. h	8. d

B.

1. c	5. b
2. a	6. a
3. b	7. c
4. c	8. c

Test 2 *(page 99)*

A.

1. just	5. possible
2. caused by	6. notice
3. followed by	7. important
4. necessary	8. hurt

B.

1. relief	5. harm
2. injury	6. damage
3. process	7. released
4. pressure	8. substances

PART 4

UNIT 1

Test 1 *(page 102)*

C.

1. c	5. a
2. b	6. b
3. c	7. a
4. a	8. c

UNIT 2

Test 2 *(page 104)*

C.

1. a	5. a
2. c	6. c
3. c	7. b
4. b	8. b

UNIT 3

Test 3 *(page 106)*

C.

1. c	5. c
2. b	6. b
3. a	7. c
4. a	8. b